RESCUE
DOGS

Crime and Rescue Canines in the Canadian Rockies

DALE PORTMAN

HERITAGE

VICTORIA · VANCOUVER · CALGARY

Heritage House Publishing Company Ltd.
www.heritagehouse.ca

Library and Archives Canada Cataloguing in Publication
Portman, Dale
    Rescue dogs: crime and rescue canines in the Canadian Rockies / Dale Portman.—1st Heritage House ed.

ISBN 978-1-894974-78-3

    1. Rescue dogs—Rocky Mountains, Canadian (B.C. and Alta.). I. Title.

SF428.55.P67 2009   636.7'0886   C2009-900072-5

First edition published 2003 by Altitude Publishing Canada Ltd.

Series editor: Lesley Reynolds.
Cover design: Chyla Cardinal. Interior design: Frances Hunter.
Cover photo: Mark Rose/iStockphoto. Interior photos: Dale Portman, except pages 13 and 23, Jasper Warden Archives; pages 34 and 86, Kananaskis Country Public Safety Archives; page 59, Banff Warden Archives; page 122, Mark Ledwidge; and author photo, Elisa Hart.

The interior of this book was printed on 100% post-consumer recycled paper, processed chlorine free and printed with vegetable-based inks

Heritage House acknowledges the financial support for its publishing program from the Government of Canada through the Canada Book Fund (CBF), Canada Council for the Arts and the province of British Columbia through the British Columbia Arts Council and the Book Publishing Tax Credit.

 Canadian Patrimoine
Heritage canadien

 Canada Council Conseil des Arts
for the Arts du Canada

 BRITISH COLUMBIA
ARTS COUNCIL

15 14 13 12 11   2 3 4 5
Printed in Canada

Dedicated to all working dogs and their handlers.
They sacrifice their time and effort for the good of all.

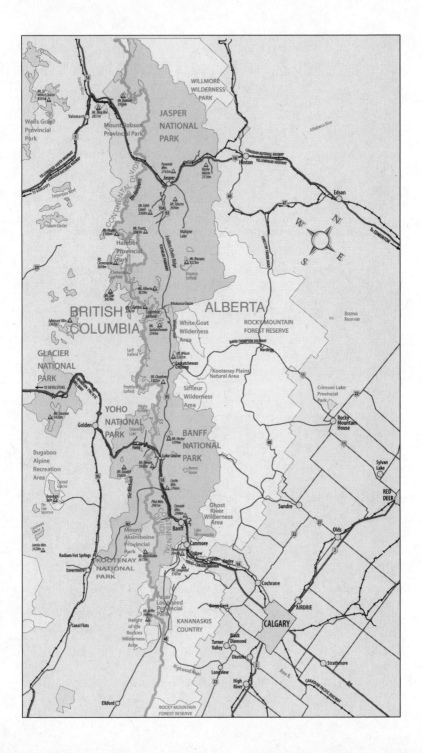

Contents

The Creation Story as Told by a Dog

On the first day of creation, God created the dog. On the second day, God created man to serve the dog. On the third day, God created all the animals of the Earth to serve as potential food for the dog. On the fourth day, God created honest toil so that man could labour for the good of the dog. On the fifth day, God created the tennis ball so that the dog might or might not retrieve it. On the sixth day, God created veterinary science to keep the dog healthy and the man broke. On the seventh day, God tried to rest, but He had to walk the dog.

—Anonymous

Prologue

SAM SITS ALERTLY AT THE *helicopter window, his ears upright, fascinated by the country passing below. He loves to work and today is no exception. Whether the work is routine or extreme, it's of little consequence to him. He leaves that up to humans to worry about. The pilot, Frank, and I watch an avalanche descend the slender ribbon of ice called Slip Stream, like a pillowy blind being drawn on a window. The slope at the bottom of this 650-metre ice route is our destination, but the avalanche is determined to reach there first. As we watch the cloud of snow spread across the slope, the radio comes alive and we hear the voice of our rescue leader. "Don't worry, boys. We've got a lookout set up in case there's another avalanche. He'll give you some warning."*

Minutes later, we land to the left of the latest avalanche on a small patch of flat ground. I kick steps in the hard snow with my ski boots. Sam scampers ahead. I have ski poles but would gladly trade them for an ice axe right now. Years earlier, a climber had been swept to his death off the ice above by a small avalanche. We had found his foot sticking out of the snow. No such signpost marks the way today as we search for two missing climbers. We are at the base of the ice, where climbers rope up, strap on crampons and pull out ice tools to start their ascent.

I look below and see the gaping chasm of a huge crevasse, like the mouth of a monstrous creature. Over the decades, many avalanches have swept down this ice route and fed this patient beast. Nearby, Frank stands by the pit he has just finished digging. It's about 1.5 metres deep and just big enough for the three of us. He dug it with the zeal of a foot soldier anticipating an artillery barrage, for this is a war zone. We have 8 to 10 seconds to reach this foxhole if or when the next avalanche comes. If the ice breaks above, the lookout in the valley will sound the alarm over the radio and we will sprint. There can be no hesitation. Not reaching the pit could mean being swept into the waiting crevasse.

There is no sign of the climbers this far up, so we slowly work our way down the slope, searching as we descend. But it's no use. After an hour and a half, we quit searching. The climbers are probably in the crevasse—and surely dead. Trying to recover the bodies at this point is too dangerous. We do not need to be added to the list of victims. Right now, we just want to get the hell out of here.

1

Alfie and Ginger: The First Team

PARK WARDEN ALFIE BURSTROM, THE first certified avalanche-dog handler in North America, now lives in retirement with his wife, June, on an acreage near Valemount, BC, surrounded by family and animals. On a page of his scrapbook is a 1964 dime that his partner, Ginger, found in an avalanche. The dog had been searching for three climbers. His find indicates how good a canine's nose can be. It also indicates how good Ginger was.

The story really started for Alfie in August 1969, at a time when he was searching for a new role in a dynamic warden service. Alfie had a speech impediment—a bad stutter—that had taken a toll on his self-esteem and comfort in dealing with people. After 15 years as a park warden, Alfie was at a low period that summer. Then Ginger came along and gave him the opportunity of a lifetime.

Alfie acquired Ginger, the runt of a litter of 11, from a fellow park warden. Ginger's father was a big German shepherd, but his mother was half coyote. At the time, the Burstrom clan lived at Decoigne Warden Station, just west of Jasper, near the Continental Divide. As a pup, Ginger accompanied Alfie's five kids on all their adventures. The kids especially liked fishing, and Ginger always went along—until he started eating their bait. To eliminate the problem, the kids would lock Ginger in the shed before heading out on a fishing trip. Hours later, their mother would come along, hear the pup whining and turn him loose. He would instantly tear around looking for their track. To the kids' consternation, Ginger would soon be in their midst, wagging his tail and looking for bait.

One of the games Alfie played with his kids was a kind of hide-and-seek. He would tell them to run as far as they could and then hide. It didn't matter whether they headed downwind or upwind. He'd then turn Ginger loose, and inevitably the pup would find them all. Alfie was unwittingly developing the dog's tracking and searching capabilities.

When Ginger was eight months old, Alfie suggested to the chief park warden that the dog was good enough to be trained as a search dog. The chief promised to look into it, and the seed of Alfie and Ginger's future was planted. Several minds within Parks Canada got together and started to look into establishing a dog program.

One man who saw the need for dogs in avalanche search and rescue was Jim Sime, the resource conservation coordinator in Calgary and the warden service's representative in regional office. Jim had already approached Parks Canada in 1969 with the idea of developing a search and rescue dog program for avalanche work. He was also aware of Alfie's speech impediment and the ridicule it brought, and that Alfie's stutter was magically gone when he talked to Ginger. As Jim put it, "Alfie was a man who had an opportunity and was seeking that opportunity, who was being downgraded and downtrodden because of his impediment, yet had a tremendous capability to bring forward."

After Jim got approval from Parks Canada to establish the dog-training program, his next step was to contact Staff Sergeant Terry Kehoe, head trainer at the RCMP Police Dog Service Training Centre at Innisfail, Alberta. As Jim explained to Kehoe, "The difference between your dogs and what I'm talking about here is that when our dog comes, it means help. It doesn't mean it's going to grab you by your backside and rip your pants off. Any dog that we have must never be trained to attack." Kehoe decided to try out Jim's idea by accepting a person selected by Parks Canada on their training course and evaluating him. Jim volunteered Alfie. Jim was gambling on Alfie and Ginger, and both men knew the future of the program depended on their success.

But Jim had faith in the pair, so Alfie went to Innisfail to qualify on the quarry course. Every day seemed like a month to Jim, who kept in touch with Kehoe, hoping for some word of encouragement. On the last day, Jim watched the final test, chewing his nails as tracker and quarry went around in circles through the course. Finally, Jim could no longer contain himself. "How did it turn out?" he cried.

"How did what turn out?" Kehoe asked.

"You know damn well what I mean! How did Alfie make out?" Jim repeated.

Kehoe replied, "You don't have another one like him, do you?" Alfie had passed with flying colours.

"You know," Jim said later with a sigh, "there was so much involved here."

Now it was Ginger's turn to be assessed at Innisfail. Before Ginger even got started, he had three strikes against him. First, he was relatively small for a working dog. Second, only one out of 80 dogs was capable of becoming a trained RCMP dog. The third issue was the matter of Ginger's coyote heritage. His breeding would be controversial until he graduated from the RCMP's dog-training school—his pedigree simply wasn't in keeping with RCMP standards for potential candidates. Coyotes were viewed as sneaky animals of prey, not loyal life companions. How dependable would Ginger be in the wilderness? Would he track a human if he scented a fresh deer track?

Kehoe was up front with Jim when they sat down to discuss Ginger a few days after he'd entered the training program. "Where in the hell did this dog come from?" he boomed.

Alfie Burstrom and Ginger.

Jim, defensive and subdued at Kehoe's brusque manner, began to whisper Ginger's history when Kehoe interrupted. "It's all right," Kehoe assured, "he's in the program."

What Jim didn't know was that the kennels had set up a special test for Ginger. Because he was to be trained as an avalanche dog, they tried to simulate that environment, digging a pit at the end of a large field where a few people hid under branches and debris. When Alfie brought Ginger out, Kehoe instructed him to turn the dog loose. Off to the left was an agility field where several dogs and their handlers were going through the course. Alfie was worried Ginger would run straight to the other dogs. Ginger, however, took off like a shot, working the wind straight to the pit to dig out the quarry. That was enough for Kehoe. Ginger was a natural.

In September 1970, Alfie and Ginger went into training for four months along with two American sheriffs. Ginger may have been a natural, but he still needed a lot of training and discipline. Alfie needed training, too. In a sense, Alfie needed to catch up to Ginger's natural ability.

In keeping with Jim's wish, Alfie and Ginger were trained in all the RCMP dog profiles except attack work. Their training also included the new avalanche search profile. In January 1971, Alfie and Ginger graduated from the RCMP training kennels as a working team, becoming the first certified avalanche search team in North America.

As soon as they started working in the field, Alfie and Ginger blossomed into an effective unit. It took longer, however, to get people on side within the warden service. The idea of using a dog on search and rescue operations or poaching cases was new to everyone there. While some readily embraced the concept, others were hesitant and doubted Ginger's abilities.

The RCMP, however, had no such doubts. From the beginning, Alfie and Ginger were in demand, getting a large share of RCMP calls from the communities surrounding Jasper. The closest RCMP dog was at Stony Plain near Edmonton, 300 kilometres away. As Alfie said, "They had me chasing God knows who. They were used to a working dog." One call from the local detachment asked for help with a hostage situation—someone was holding an RCMP officer hostage with a rifle. The RCMP hoped that Alfie and Ginger could alleviate the explosive situation.

Alfie's bluff was on. He cautiously approached with Ginger until they were a reasonable distance from the hostage taker and the Mountie. Suddenly, the rifle was trained on Alfie and Ginger. "This dog will tear you to pieces," said Alfie. Ginger, seemingly on cue, jumped and barked. "All he wanted to do was lick him," Alfie said later. The hostage taker yelled that he would shoot Alfie, to which Alfie replied, "If you do that, the dog will tear you apart, and if you shoot the dog, you won't get another round in the rifle."

Alfie was unarmed, but he had an RCMP officer as backup with his gun cocked and ready. In fact, he said, the gun "was damn near resting on my shoulder." The bluff worked, and Alfie and Ginger's reputation grew.

With the success Alfie and Ginger were having in the field, it wasn't long before Banff National Park took notice. In 1973, Banff decided to join the program and sent candidates to the training kennels for evaluation. Soon, two more warden dog teams were working in the field—Earl Skjonsberg in Banff and Jack Woledge in Lake Louise. Because of Alfie's experiences working with the RCMP, the teams were later trained in the criminal apprehension and attack profile. Since then, the program has successfully spread to other national parks in Canada.

For Jim Sime, one of the biggest rewards in his long and distinguished career with Parks Canada was helping Alfie and Ginger. It was also one of his biggest gambles. Jim believes that the program's success rested on Alfie and Ginger. He reflects, "It's just a gift, that dog. The guy and the dog had been brought together, and they deeply respected each other."

Alfie and Ginger worked together for 11 years. Ginger remained fit and active to the end. The team was featured in numerous newspaper articles, and their story has appeared in elementary-school textbooks across Canada. In the early 1970s, they were also featured in a CBC special on Jasper. They were a highly respected team among other RCMP dog handlers. Indeed, in the Canadian Rockies, Alfie and Ginger were number one.

2

Avalanche on Mt. Edith Cavell

THERE COMES A TIME WHEN a handler and dog must prove their worth to everyone they work with. It always seems that when a working dog performs brilliantly, nobody is around to see the results. When the dog makes a mistake, everybody seems to be paying attention. However, each team usually has its defining moment. For Alfie and Ginger, that moment was when Ginger found a single dime in the chaos of an avalanche site.

On February 19, 1972, a party of four from the Alpine Club of Canada's Edmonton chapter—Pete Ford, Jim Carlson, Wayne Smith and Chris Smith—left for Mt. Edith Cavell, in Jasper National Park. They had registered out at 8:00 a.m. for an ascent of the mountain via the east ridge.

The group was planning to climb the mountain, get back down and ski out to the highway by midnight of the next day. Their return date was listed as February 21 at 12:00 a.m.

Parking their car at the beginning of Cavell Road, the foursome was met by a local outfitter, who towed the group by snowmobile the 15 kilometres up the unplowed road to the teahouse. From the teahouse, they skied up the valley, under the mountain's imposing north face. The Angel Glacier spread her wings over the lower stretch of the face, while a prominent lateral moraine rose steeply to the group's left. Just beyond the moraine was a timbered ridge, its summit crowned by a beautiful and expansive alpine prairie known as Cavell Meadows.

The party reached the base of the saddle at the head of the valley. They left their skis here as the snow up to the saddle was hard and more easily travelled by kicking steps. Once they reached the saddle, they swung right and up a slope that grew increasingly steeper. They continued up a broad, snow-filled gully that would eventually put them near the east ridge proper.

At the top of the gully, the group decided to dig a snow cave for the night. This would provide a cozy, moderately warm abode and get them out of the wind. It was 5:00 p.m. when they started to dig a few metres from the top. A warm front had moved in during the day, raising temperatures above freezing and shrouding the group in cloud.

Pete remembers completing the cave and crawling

inside. Unbeknownst to the group, the change in weather had disastrously weakened the slope where they had built the cave. There was a loud crack and the snow cave collapsed. Pete was knocked flat on his face by the weight of the roof on top of him, and he found himself pinned to the hard snow beneath. Certain his chest would be crushed, he thought, "What a horrible way to die." Suddenly, he was in motion, moving headfirst downhill. He tried to dig his elbows into the snow to bring his head up, but with no luck.

The slide travelled downhill over a hard layer in the snowpack, speeding up as it disintegrated. There was nothing anyone caught in the avalanche could do. The four climbers were being carried down to the saddle, 600 metres below. Witnesses to the avalanche might have heard the whoosh of air as the slope settled. Cracks appeared on the snow's surface, spiderwebbing out in all directions.

Pete came to rest after flying over a rock buttress in the middle of the gully. He was pinned headfirst with his upper body jammed in the snow and his legs on the surface. Knowing that avalanche debris sets like concrete, he frantically wrenched his body clear of the snow. He found himself in fresh snow by a large rock to one side of the main avalanche deposit. When he tried to get to his feet, he realized one arm was broken near the elbow. He remembers no pain, just numbness. Pete's climbing partners were not so fortunate.

As Pete moved toward the avalanche debris, he saw Jim, who cried, "Help me dig my leg out and I'll help to look

for the others." But when Pete reached his friend, he realized Jim's leg was bent at an unnatural angle, and he would
be incapable of moving on his own. Pete then turned his
thoughts to Wayne and Chris. The avalanche debris was
about 70 metres wide and 100 metres long, a substantial
area to search. After a cursory look, Pete found no evidence
of Wayne and Chris and returned to Jim. He splinted Jim's
broken leg to his good one, slid him into a sleeping bag and
piled packs, clothing and snow around him. Then Pete left
to get help.

It was now 8:00 p.m. and totally dark. Night had settled
on the mountain, intensifying Pete's feelings of isolation at
the desperate situation. His skis were at the bottom of the
hill, but with a broken arm, it would be difficult to ski, so he
took only one ski pole. He dug around in a pack and pulled
out a container of liquid honey and a headlamp. With some
difficulty, Pete managed to follow the route they'd taken
on the way up, hearing a number of stony avalanches as he
picked his way back down the gully.

Eventually, Pete reached the deserted teahouse. He had
been hoping to find a telephone, but found nothing. Sitting
in the pit toilet for shelter, he swallowed some honey and
then continued down the mountain. But in the gloom of the
night, Pete missed the road out and took a route that led to
Cavell Lake instead. The deep snow made for slow going,
and Pete often had to move forward by lying on his back
and pushing himself along with his legs and ski pole, his

broken arm resting on his thigh. While the detour didn't add much in terms of distance, it cost Pete an hour or two—and much more in energy and hardship. If there was any chance of saving his friends, Pete needed to get out as soon as possible.

Finally, he reached the far end of Cavell Lake. He then followed a road that connected with Cavell Road—but from there it was still 13 kilometres to the highway. He walked through the night, forcing himself to keep moving. The going was better if he managed to stay on the part of the road packed by snowmobile traffic, but he often slipped off, sinking to his hips in the deep snow. Exhausted from his physical exertion and the pain of his broken arm, Pete sometimes fell asleep while walking, collapsing in the snow. Finally, dawn broke, and it was easier, although discouraging, to see the road winding ahead. But the need to get help for his friends kept Pete going.

Shortly before noon, Pete reached the car. Thankful that he had an automatic, he headed for the warden station a few kilometres south on Highway 93A. At 12:10 p.m., Shirley Klettl was surprised to see Pete at the back door, haggard and exhausted. Shirley, wife of veteran warden Tony Klettl, sprang into action. She quickly went to the wooden forestry phone hanging on the wall and gave a crank on the handle, sending one long ring to the fire hall. Soon she was talking to the chief park warden, Bud Armstrong, giving him the details. She also spoke to the park's alpine specialist,

Willi Pfisterer, who was at Marmot Basin conducting some avalanche control work in the ski area. Willi asked Pete to drive back to the start of Cavell Road to meet with the rescue team.

The warden service leaped into action, calling wardens in from several districts throughout the park. In all, 12 wardens responded, and by 1:15 p.m., they had gathered at the staging area and were geared up and ready to go. Meanwhile, a rescue helicopter was dispatched from Hinton, Alberta.

Willi, the rescue leader, interviewed Pete at the staging area and later recalled, "He was really bashed up with a broken arm, and I asked him some questions and he precisely answered them . . . He gave clear answers and I knew exactly what had happened and where it was. So the thing to do was to get there as fast as possible—because of the light."

The helicopter had arrived but was grounded until 2:30 p.m. because of bad weather. When the clouds lifted, Willi and two wardens immediately took off to do a reconnaissance. In the meantime, a team of wardens travelled up Cavell Road by snowmobile and established an advanced rescue base at the teahouse. When the helicopter flew above the saddle, Willi could see a prone figure on the surface of the avalanche debris—Jim. There was room to land the helicopter on the slide deposit, and at 3:00 p.m. they confirmed that Jim was dead. He appeared to have died of internal injuries rather than exposure. And because rigor mortis had set in, the rescuers concluded he'd been dead for some time.

Alfie Burstrom and Ginger prepare to lift off under a helicopter at Jasper National Park.

They decided to get Alfie Burstrom and his search dog, Ginger, flown to the site, as well as Sergeant Al Moore, who would act as the RCMP coroner. While waiting for the dog team, Willi and the two wardens started a hasty search of the deposit, looking for signs of the other two victims. While they conducted their search, the weather deteriorated again. Alfie, Ginger and Sergeant Moore waited out the storm at the teahouse. Willi realized it had been a mistake not to have flown Alfie and Ginger in on the initial flight.

At 4:00 p.m., the weather improved and the helicopter was able to land at the avalanche site. Alfie put Ginger to work, and immediately the dog ran to the dead body. When Alfie got to the deposit, the first thing he heard was, "Get that damn dog out of here." As much as the comment upset him, Alfie didn't want to start a row—he needed to get Ginger back to work.

Because this was one of the first corpses Ginger had experienced, he was curious. Alfie allowed him to investigate, then moved him farther up the deposit to search for the victims under the snow. But Ginger was distracted by the climber's gear, which was scattered about on the surface. Most search dogs are trained to indicate anything with human scent on it, and there was an abundance of things littered about there—pots, clothing, bivouac sacs and so on. Ginger would return with an article, expecting praise, and Alfie would have to acknowledge it, giving Ginger a pat and a

"Good boy" before sending him back to work. This process took time, and time is critical in avalanche searches. Soon, though, Ginger ignored the surface articles, which didn't elicit much reaction from his handler, and sniffed for something beneath the snow.

Willi had his own concerns. Time was running out. If they didn't find Wayne and Chris in the next hour, a camp was going to have to be flown in and set up nearby—with the current weather conditions, he couldn't rely on flying back the next morning. Willi looked up at Alfie and Ginger, working across the deposit. This was the first time he'd had to depend on the team. He hoped Ginger would come through soon, for everyone's sake—someone could still be alive under the snow.

Willi was also concerned about Alfie. Because this was the team's first avalanche search, Willi knew that Alfie was feeling pressure. The longer the team searched without a result, the higher Alfie's anxiety level would rise, which would be picked up by Ginger. And who knew how the dog would respond? A dog as a search tool needed to be sold to those in the search and rescue field, and there were many skeptics among the wardens themselves. Willi knew a failure here would affect Alfie and Ginger's confidence and could possibly set the whole dog program back.

Alfie knew there were two people left in the deposit, unless they had lodged somewhere above or been thrown clear of the slide. Looking up the gully, it seemed unlikely that either had happened. Alfie felt the scrutiny he and his dog were under.

It was 5:00 p.m., and Ginger had been searching for 40 minutes without any sign of finding a victim. Trying to hide his concern, Willi called, "How's the dog working, Alfie?"

"Oh, fine," replied Alfie in a relaxed fashion not befitting the situation. "We found the first one a half hour ago." This was a surprise—and relief—to Willi.

"That's great, Alfie, really great," he called back. "Thank the dog for me."

Alfie had kept silent when Ginger found Wayne's body because he didn't need a coroner to tell him he was dead. But he also didn't want the other searchers tracking up the area and creating a distraction for the dog. There was another reason. He didn't like being told to get his dog off the avalanche, as though Ginger was nothing more than a family pet. He was upset about the comment and felt little cohesion with his fellow searchers at the moment.

Finding one body removed some of the pressure, but stress remained in the search party below as darkness loomed and there was still a chance of a survivor. Soon, Ginger started digging in one spot, an indication that something was buried there. It was a dime. Ginger's nose was definitely at work.

Alfie gradually moved Ginger into the area where Wayne's body had been found. Suddenly, the dog started digging frantically, his tail wagging. Shortly afterwards, he barked and then growled. Ginger had found Chris' body. By the time Alfie reached the dog, Ginger was tugging on the dead climber's sleeve. Alfie responded with customary encouragement, "Good boy. That a boy. You get him out of there."

It was 5:45 p.m., and although both climbers were dead, Willi gave a sigh of relief. The dog team had come through, and everybody would be off the mountain that night. The evacuation by helicopter started at 6:15 p.m., with personnel and bodies being removed first, followed by the camp gear. The rescue operation was completed by 8:30 p.m.

Pete now lives in Canmore, Alberta. Over the years, the memory of this tragedy has been a burden. The loss of good friends is not something easily forgotten. When fate dictates that you are the only survivor of such an accident, your life seems to take on an added weight. Pete remains active and enthusiastic in mountain pursuits, recently completing a rafting trip on the Nahanni River in the Northwest Territories.

With this 1972 rescue, the warden service entered a new era, with dogs becoming an integral part of search and rescue in the Canadian Rockies.

CHAPTER

3

A Tragic Photograph
of the Maligne Canyon

IN THE SIX KILOMETRES FROM the Maligne Canyon tea-house to the junction of the Athabasca River, six bridges cross the Maligne River. All but one are footbridges, and all but two are suspended high over the torrential water racing through the canyon. In some places, the canyon walls are so close that, if you were athletic, you could jump from one side to the other. The trail that follows the river is one of the most interesting in Jasper National Park, but it's a trail with a tragic past.

The tragedy unfolded in 1971 on a hot summer day that started innocently enough. A nine-year-old girl was directed backwards for a photograph—her parents wanted the Maligne River to be in the background—but she

28

stepped back too far and fell into the river. The strong current grabbed her, carrying her swiftly downstream and into the walled confines of the canyon. Within seconds, she was swept over the first waterfall.

Once the alarm sounded, all the wardens in the area rushed to the bridge sites along the trail. They knew it was unlikely that anyone could survive a trip through the canyon—let alone the fall—but that didn't deter them. The wardens moved quickly, hoping for a miracle.

I was called in to patrol the canyon walls in the hope of finding the girl alive, possibly clinging to some wedged driftwood or perched on a ledge. Peering into the abyss of roaring falls and churning black pools, I knew this to be a very remote chance. It was my third summer as a seasonal park warden and my first experience of an accident of this magnitude. Because of these circumstances, the incident remains fixed in my mind.

Alfie Burstrom, the dog handler stationed at Jasper, was aware of the rescue in progress and was puzzled that no one had called for him and his dog, Ginger. He hung around the radio all day, waiting for a request for help. Late that night, the phone finally rang. They wanted Alfie on site early the next morning. Alfie and Ginger were Parks Canada's first and only trained dog team. At the time, it was a constant battle to remind people of their worth, or even that they existed. Alfie hoped the call meant that people were finally buying into the program.

He showed up at first light with Ginger, eager to go. To his dismay, the rescue leader wanted him to rappel into the canyon at strategic places to look for the missing girl. The rescue leader saw no use for the dog in this operation and was surprised when Alfie retorted, "Screw your search if you don't want to use the dog!" Alfie was going to do things his way.

Alfie was determined to use Ginger. He decided to search the river's edge below the sixth bridge, close to where the Maligne enters the Athabasca. He informed the rescue leader of his plan. The rescue leader reconsidered and as an afterthought sent me with them. "Here's a man, use him wisely!" he yelled, as Alfie and Ginger stormed off.

I felt like a pawn in a wilderness soap opera—I played the fresh-faced seasonal warden, eager for anything. I caught up to the handler and his dog and heard Alfie spewing out a cloud of profanity that would have been the envy of any cowpoke pushing stubborn cattle. I took up the rear, trying to be as inconspicuous as possible. Alfie wasn't a tall man, but he was big in a skookum sort of way, and I certainly didn't want to get in his path.

I searched along the bank of the river to where it enters the Athabasca, a distance of about half a kilometre. The bank was deeply undercut, making it difficult to see anything in the water. Warden Max Winkler searched on the opposite shore. Alfie and Ginger were working along the river when Ginger stopped and peered into the water. Alfie couldn't see anything and tried to move on, but Ginger returned to the spot and again looked into the moving water. He stared at the water, looked over at Alfie, then stared again at the water.

Alfie got down on his hands and knees and peered beneath the bank. Below the surface of the water he saw something white that looked like a hand. He called Max and me over, and Max offered to go in to investigate. Alfie secured a rope around him, and Max backed into the river. He was soon up to his chest in icy water. He felt clothing, then an arm, and after a bit of struggling he managed to free the body from a tangle of roots. We had found the girl.

Although it was a body recovery, not a rescue, Alfie believed his mission was a success. Ginger had proved why a dog was needed, and Alfie wanted to let everyone know. In the early years of the dog program, it was important to establish when dogs could be used and how effective they were.

Ginger's success was also important because it was the first time in Canada that a dog had found anybody underwater. Before long, the RCMP Police Dog Service Training Centre in Innisfail was experimenting with the concept. They found that warm, stagnant water tends to mask human odour, while cold, clear water allows the gases from the body to rise to the surface, where they are more readily detected by dogs. Because virtually all water in the Canadian Rockies is cold and clear, the use of dogs on river searches quickly became an important tool.

This search and Ginger's recovery of bodies from the 1972 Mt. Edith Cavell avalanche helped prove the value of dogs for emergency response teams, and there was soon a need for more dog handlers. Inspired by Alfie and Ginger, I became a dog handler in the fall of 1981 and worked alongside Alfie for several years. Gord Peyto, in Glacier/ Revelstoke, and Scott Ward, in Banff, came up through the ranks with me. Together, we helped take the dog program further in its evolution.

4

Hector Lake Drowning

IN THE LATE 1980S, Parks Canada dog handlers and their RCMP counterparts started training their dogs in lake searches. One of the first such searches took place in July 1991, when Warden Gord Peyto and his dog, Baron, were called to a drowning at Hector Lake. Baron was a Belgian Melanois, a breed that had been used extensively for police work in eastern Europe with excellent results. Melanois are smaller and redder than German shepherds. Baron was so small that I used to say he was nothing more than a squirrel on steroids. But he was a super working dog and a natural as a water-search dog.

Gord had originally been called out from Golden, BC, for a crevasse search on Mt. Victoria, but was diverted to

A river rescue in Kananaskis Country.

Hector Lake. The night before, two people canoeing in the frigid lake had overturned. One made it to shore to report the accident. Unless the second person had somehow swam to shore at some remote location, Gord knew the job was likely a body recovery.

When Gord and Baron arrived, the rescue team had been looking all night with no success. On reaching the lakeshore, Baron went to work. Hector Lake is big, and if the body wasn't close to shore, there would be no chance for Baron to pick up the scent. But as the dog worked the water's edge, an offshore breeze carried a scent to his nose. He lifted his head and ran along the shore, back and forth, until he was satisfied something was out there. Without warning, Baron jumped into the lake and started swimming. Gord ran for a canoe and cast off in pursuit of his dog.

Baron was swimming in a shallow zigzag out into the lake. He paddled furiously, his head raised with his nose scenting the air current, like a seal balancing a ball. He then started paddling in a tight circle. Around and around he went in the same spot until Gord arrived in the canoe. As he approached, the dog started barking.

Gord threw a marker buoy out at the spot, retrieved Baron and paddled back to shore. Now they could concentrate their search. From the canoe, you could see less than a metre beneath the surface because of the glacial silt suspended in the water—in such lakes, it's easier to see objects below the surface from directly above. With this in mind, the search team requested a flyby using the rescue helicopter.

From above the site Baron had indicated, the body could be seen about two metres from the marker buoy, but they could not determine how deep it was, so a dive team investigated. They searched the area for several hours, but the visibility underwater was less than a metre, and they came up with nothing. To this day, the body has never been recovered and remains in its watery grave.

5

Hoods in the Woods

IT WAS NOON ON MARCH 15, 1987, and I had stopped at Hillsdale Meadows, west of Banff, to run my dog, Sam. We were alone until three vehicles pulled into the small parking lot. It was a group planning to snowshoe in the area, and we chatted for a while. One of the party told me he had seen a fellow in camouflage clothing with a hunting bow near the roadside a few kilometres toward Banff. Because hunting is illegal in a national park, he had my attention.

Driving east to where the man had been spotted, I flagged down two bicyclists coming toward me. They said they'd seen three men in camouflage clothing near the road. To them, it looked like the men were carrying rifles, not bows. With this new information, I knew I had to be cautious.

I immediately got on the radio, informing warden dispatch in Banff of my location and requesting backup, including the RCMP. As I continued east, I requested that the dog handler from Banff, Scott Ward, be sent out with his dog, Gypsy. Wardens Peter Enderwick and Al Westhaver were also en route. Dispatch radioed back saying that the RCMP officers were tied up and couldn't come yet.

I drove another few kilometres and came upon a small red car parked in a pull-off. As I approached, the driver flashed his headlights a couple of times. Maybe he had car trouble, I thought. I drove up to the vehicle, rolled down my window, and asked the occupant if he was having problems. He said no, but he was wearing camouflage clothing, which put me on alert. As I looked past him, I saw a bow and some arrows partially concealed under a coat on the seat. Why had he flashed his headlights if there wasn't a problem? My truck was well marked as a peace-officer vehicle, with a red and blue light bar on the roof. He seemed to want to draw me in for some reason, and it was unsettling.

I radioed the licence-plate number and a description of the vehicle, then stepped out of my truck and asked him where his friends were. He said they were walking around in the bush. In response to my questions, he told me they were carrying bows. I then heard a shot coming from the bush across the road. It sounded like a .22. It didn't seem to be aimed in our direction, but that was of little consolation.

My voice rose as I asked, "Does that sound like a bow and arrow?" Things were getting tense. I demanded, "How many rifles do they have? What are the calibres, and how many of them are there?"

He quickly answered, "Three people, four rifles, all .22s."

I called Peter, informing him of the shot, and asked him to push the speed limit in getting there. At that point, I pulled my rifle out and dug up my ammunition. I put the clip in place and laid it next to me on the seat. Al had requested a vehicle history from dispatch on the suspect's car and made a follow-up request for RCMP backup. Banff dispatch contacted Constable Fred Martens, who left immediately from Lake Louise. Constable Hardy of the RCMP detachment in Field, BC, was also on his way.

I removed the bow and arrows from the suspect's vehicle, confiscated his car keys and returned to my truck. Throughout all this, Sam barked periodically from his vantage point in the back of the truck. Usually this is annoying, especially when you're trying to talk to someone, but it was comforting at the time. The driver had asked about the dog earlier, and I emphasized he was a police dog, fully capable of attacking someone if necessary.

Then I heard the rapid fire of a semi-automatic rifle or automatic pistol and instinctively ducked by my vehicle. It was about seven or eight rounds, and again it wasn't directed our way. Nonetheless, I got back in my truck. Because it was facing the car, I could keep an eye on the driver as well as the area of bush where I'd heard the shots come from. My hand rested on the rifle at my side.

Peter and Al arrived shortly after that. A minute later, Warden Tom Davidson arrived, but stayed farther down the road, where he could use his binoculars to survey the area toward the bush. After I updated all of them, Al parked 200 metres up the road and put on his emergency lights. Peter dealt with the driver. Sam was now making a huge commotion in the truck. He could sense that something was up and wanted to get involved.

My plan was to track the group in the bush, but not until I had RCMP backup with some weapons. While I waited, Peter searched the driver and car, finding a loaded .22 rifle in the back seat. About then, Scott arrived with Gypsy, and I briefed him. Dispatch called with instructions that none of us were to enter the bush until RCMP backup were on the scene.

Around 45 minutes after it had all started, Constable Fred Martens and Assistant Chief Park Warden John Steele arrived. I asked Martens to accompany me on the track and got the excited Sam out of the truck. The driver had given me a rough idea where the other three had walked into the bush, and I felt we had a good chance of finding them.

No sooner were we ready to start than three men walked out of the bush 200 metres away and came toward us. To say we were surprised is an understatement. They were told to put their hands behind their head. Sam was going nuts, barking and whining as the group approached. Body searches revealed a loaded 9 mm handgun in one man's shoulder holster and a loaded Colt .45 in another's waistband—these guys were heavily armed. Apparently, they had seen Sam from their hiding spot and had decided to turn themselves in. Because none of the men had any rifles, there was a good possibility they had been stashed somewhere in the bush. I intended to find them, with Sam's help.

We decided that Scott would accompany me as backup, leaving Gypsy in the truck. By now, Constable Hardy had arrived from Field and taken custody of the suspects. I cast Sam around in the ditch, and after one pass he had something. Soon he was locked onto the track and we were off, crashing through the bush.

We ducked and dodged as I clasped the end of the line. Sam was tearing along with pent-up excitement, and I was trying to check him. The last thing I wanted to do was trip, which can happen easily when you're being pulled by a dog. You're so focused on the animal that you don't pay enough attention to where your feet are landing. I also didn't want to miss the cache of rifles, but it was as if Sam had his throttle button stuck on full. At least I had the line to hang on to. Scott had to work hard to keep up. Fortunately, he was a long-distance runner and used to running behind a dog.

In less than five minutes, we'd found their campsite. Nothing of immediate interest turned up, so I cast Sam around and picked up the track again. Eventually, Sam

Warden-service dog handlers with working dogs. From left to right: Dale Portman and Sam, Alfie Burstrom and Hiko, Scott Ward and Gypsy, and Gord Peyto and Saxon.

found several rounds of .22 ammunition and a bottle of alcohol. A little farther along, he found a concealed bag with tools and shovels—but still no rifles. We decided to search back along the track to the campsite in case they had concealed the rifles somewhere along the route, but nothing of importance turned up. We found lots of spent cartridges, but no rifles. Agreeing to end the search, Scott and I returned to the vehicles, where I kennelled Sam in my truck.

All the suspects except the unarmed one were then

transported to the RCMP detachment in Banff. John, Constable Hardy, Tom, the suspect, Scott and I walked to the campsite to collect the evidence. We then gathered what Sam had found near the road and returned to the vehicles. We'd found a lot of good evidence, but where were those rifles I'd heard earlier?

Because the rifles were still missing, Scott took Gypsy, who was fresher than Sam, out of the truck and walked her over to where the threesome had left the bush. He turned her loose and worked her farther along the road from where Sam had searched. Before long, she found the rifles in a low depression, where they had been covered with snow. We now had ample evidence for the criminal charges that would follow.

What had started as a casual conversation with some park visitors turned out to be one of the more interesting episodes of crime detection in Sam's career. All four men were convicted of weapons charges under both the Criminal Code and the National Parks Act. Their weapons were turned over to the Crown, and they received heavy fines. The men, in their late teens and early 20s, were from Vancouver and had no understanding of national parks or that firearms were prohibited—they were simply testing their weapons and practising their survival skills.

Although the outcome was successful, everyone involved in the incident agreed that the potential for disaster had been great. If the suspects hadn't been as docile as they were, the results could have been much different. As I was the only armed officer at the scene, we were seriously outgunned.

There is one question, however, that remains unanswered to this day. Why had the driver flashed his headlights at me when I arrived? Did he want to be found? Was he uneasy about his involvement with the other three and looking for a way out? I will likely never know.

CHAPTER

6

Rescue on the
Endless Chain

A GOOD DOG HANDLER IS SENSITIVE to his dog's body
language, able to differentiate between what's important
and what's not. To be successful in the field, a handler must
constantly observe and evaluate his dog's unique signs.
But a handler can't watch the dog all the time—sometimes
noticing a sign that can make the difference between life
and death is a matter of luck—or fate. So it was at Sunwapta
Falls one cold, snowy July afternoon in 1987.

A young couple who worked at Sunwapta Falls
Bungalows, south of Jasper, had gone for a late-afternoon
hike and hadn't returned that night. The next morning,
I drove out with my dog, Sam, and met Warden Art
Lawrenson. Art worked as a seasonal warden out of the

Poboktan Warden Station, up the highway from Sunwapta Falls. It was his first summer in the field.

Art and I spoke to the manager of the bungalows, then another staff member pointed out a cliff outcropping across the valley, on the lower slopes of the Endless Chain Ridge. He said the couple had last been seen there, sitting on the rocks like marmots snoozing in the afternoon sun. As Art and I assessed the situation, a few drops of rain started to fall. We now had a last-seen point, so we hiked across the valley up to the cliff to see if Sam could pick anything up.

When we got to the outcropping, I slipped Sam's tracking harness over his head and fastened it around his chest. The harness distributes the pull on the line evenly around the dog's shoulders, much like a sled-dog harness. I then clipped into it with a 6-metre leather tracking line. I cast him in a big arc over the rough ground, trying to pick up a track. After a couple of passes, he caught a scent and his head swung back to investigate. He had something. We were off. But minutes later, the track was gone and Sam frantically cast about. Again, he picked up the scent and off we went, only for him to lose it again. The track was just too old. We worked it for more than an hour, picking up less and less, until finally the scent was gone altogether.

The track Sam had been piecing together was leading uphill toward a ridge, so we continued to walk through the trees in that direction until we broke out into a clearing. We were now in upper subalpine, more open terrain than farther down in the valley. I again cast Sam around, trying to pick up a track, but there was nothing. Deciding to continue up, Art and I angled toward a prominent ridge. By this time, the rain was getting heavier. Because there was no scent, we looked for any visual sign of passage, such as a dislodged rock or a footprint.

When we broke into the alpine zone, leaving trees behind, the rain turned to snow. As we continued climbing, the snow intensified and started to settle on the ground. The landscape was now white where moments before it had been green and gold with splashes of red, purple and yellow from alpine flowers. It was wet, heavy snow. Each snowflake was so large it seemed to cast a shadow. The footing turned slippery as the soft carpet of moss and lichen gave way to smooth-faced, snow-plastered rock. Conditions worsened when the wind picked up.

My thoughts went to the overdue couple. If they were still high up on the mountain, they would find themselves in difficult straits with this snow. If they didn't have adequate protective clothing, the situation could be life-threatening.

As we climbed, the terrain got steeper, and we soon found ourselves on slabby rock that was treacherous with the snow. Even Sam kept slipping. I was ready to call off the search and turn around. Going on seemed pointless—there were no indications the couple had gone this way. We were clutching at straws. We finally stopped at a break in the rock, and as a last resort, I gave a couple of yells, then listened for an answer. When none came, I turned to start climbing down—until I noticed Sam. He was looking up the mountain, ears cocked, while slowly angling his head back and forth. He seemed to hear something we couldn't. I pointed this out to Art, who looked at Sam with both puzzlement and hope.

It was enough to convince me to continue. But it was rough going for Sam, so I tied him to a rock and left him. Art and I pushed on over the slick rock. After about 15 minutes, we stopped and yelled again. We were going to have to turn around soon as we were getting into terrain where we would need a climbing rope to continue. The wind was a constant companion, slapping loose pack straps in our faces as we strained to hear something. Finally, over the sound of the wind, we detected a faint echo. Someone was calling for help. We had found them.

Unfortunately, the couple was still a considerable way up the mountain—we would probably need a rescue team to retrieve them. I radioed for help and carefully climbed down to where I had left Sam, leaving Art where he was.

Time was now critical. The weather had turned nasty, it was late in the afternoon and few hours of daylight remained. Even if they were dressed properly, it would be a challenge for the lost couple to make it through another night in the storm. There was also a good possibility that one or both of them were injured. Sam and I had done all we could, so we hiked down the mountain to a spot the helicopter could possibly fly to with the rescue team.

After I left, Art was determined to reach the couple. He slowly worked his way up until he got close to them. They were in the middle of a huge limestone slab, snuggled together like the last vestige of plant life clinging to some protected niche. It was about a 40- or 50-degree slope, and Art found a crack that he could work his way up until he was about eight or nine metres from them. The slab was covered in wet, slimy snow, and he could go no farther without slipping off himself. There was a cliff below him that added to the danger; a fall could have been fatal. Art got on the radio and relayed the information to the base rescue leader, who was in the process of dispatching a team by helicopter.

The snow was coming in horizontally as Art tried to comfort the couple and keep their spirits up. His presence alone was a big boost for them. They were wearing only basic gear, with windbreakers covering their light clothing and no gloves or toques—nothing that could keep the elements out. The couple had spent the night farther along the crest near the summit and had travelled that morning until they'd reached this point. When it became too dangerous to navigate the steep rock, they waited, calling out for help at intervals. It was the smartest thing they could have done.

To Art, it seemed a long time before he heard the helicopter. I directed it in with two wardens attached at the end

Dale Portman with Sam.

of the sling rope. It was 3:00 p.m. when wardens Pat Sheehan and Greg Horne were gently deposited at the site where I was waiting. After I briefed them, they headed up the ridge. It took them the better part of an hour to reach Art and the young couple. When I heard on the radio that Pat and Greg had reached Art, Sam and I headed down the mountain to the bungalows.

When Pat and Greg got to the scene, they realized they would have to climb above the couple, then lower a rope to them—it was too steep and slippery to approach from below. Greg lowered Pat, who put the pair in harnesses. Then Greg rappelled down and joined them. They crab-walked the couple across the slab to the edge and down to a bigger ledge near Art. This took well over an hour because the two hikers were hypothermic and could barely move.

Art was also becoming hypothermic, shivering like crazy. Pat told him to take his warden's Stetson off and put his hood over his head, but by then Art was so cold he wasn't responding. Pat finally pulled the hat off Art's head, prompting him to pull up his hood. They had to get moving.

Pat took the young woman in hand, and Art guided the young man, while Greg brought up the rear with all the gear. They roped the couple down through the steep rock, but it was a slow, tedious process. Art remembers giving directions such as, "Put your foot here. Put your foot there. Let's go over to this rock. Let's go over that way. Hold my hand. Slide down on your bum on this one and I'll catch you." They entered a boulder field that Art later said was "like climbing through a junkyard of greasy refrigerators and Volkswagens." On top of this, they were constantly fighting the wind and driving snow.

By the time they reached the spot where Greg and Pat had slung in, the weather was completely socked in. It was now 5:00 p.m. Although it had finally stopped snowing, waves of clouds kept rolling up the slope. They desperately needed the helicopter to remove the hikers in the sling, but the pilot was hampered by near-zero visibility. They could hear the helicopter inching up the ridge, and Pat guided the pilot by radio: "More to the left. More to the right— you're directly below us," like some kind of voice braille. Eventually, the helicopter and the trailing sling rope materialized out of the swirling clouds.

Pat was worried about the young woman, who seemed to be the most hypothermic, so she slung out on the first flight with Art. Art himself was becoming less and less coherent as the cold penetrated his body. Greg and the young man were slung out next, and Pat flew out last. To guide him back to the retrieval site on each return trip, Todd McCready, the pilot, had found a gully to the right of the ridge that he used as a signpost. It was perilous flying, adding another epic dimension to the rescue.

During the flight out, the young man's body had cooled dramatically, and his core temperature had plummeted by the time he reached the parking lot. He was passing into unconsciousness. The couple was quickly packed into the waiting ambulance and taken to Jasper.

Art remembers watching all this. He should have gone to the hospital also, but he was in a different category. He was a rescuer. He remembers having numerous bowls of scalding soup and hot chocolate and going over the day's events. It was exciting and one of his first rescues. It was the first time he had worked with a dog and been slung under a helicopter in a real situation.

The couple recovered fully and soon returned to work. Art would always remember the incident as the "sling rescue in the clouds." He also recalls that it took days before he felt like he had warmed up.

Several factors saved the young couple's lives: the fact that they remained at their perch, Art's perseverance and the presence of a helicopter and rescue team. But we might never have found them in the first place had it not been for Sam's keen sense of hearing. He became a bit of a hero in Jasper after that. Even the local paper declared, SAM HAS A NOSE FOR TROUBLE.

CHAPTER

7

Avalanche on Mt. Columbia —Or Was It Mt. Bryce?

IN THE FADING DAYLIGHT OF June 14, 1987, Corporal Bland of the British Army found himself the only one of a party of four unscathed in an avalanche accident—a training program gone horribly wrong. He didn't know where he was in relation to the sea of mountains that stretched wave after wave ahead of him. All he knew—or thought he knew—was that he was on Mt. Columbia, on the western edge of the Columbia Icefield. He had no map and no understanding of the country. The only place he could go was down.

Bland watched his feet closely as he crossed a boulder field. He had reached a ridge and could see a river, Bryce Creek, winding through a dark valley far below. Since it offered the best chance of finding help, he was determined to reach it—never mind the fact that it was kilometres away and there was no road or trail to lead him there.

As luck would have it, Bland chose to go down the right side of the ridge. If he'd gone to his left, an impassable canyon would have blocked him. And if that had happened, his journey out would have been extended by days. As it was, he spent most of the night negotiating the difficult terrain in the darkness, trying to reach Bryce Creek. There was great urgency in his endeavour, for after the avalanche he had seen someone stirring on the debris far below, but it had been impossible to climb down the ice slope from where he was. But he had to be careful. He would be no good to anyone if he broke a leg on the way out.

Toward dawn, Bland finally reached the main drainage, where he travelled easily for several kilometres on the gravel flats. However, when the river entered the forest, with its deadfall, darkness and devil's club, a spiny shrub, his progress slowed considerably. Eventually, Bland saw a clearing off in the distance on a mountainside. He could tell it had been cut down for logging, and his hopes soared as he made for the clearing. As he drew closer, he heard chainsaws, and his pace quickened in their direction. To his relief, he found three men clearing trees. Shakily approaching them, Bland told them his story and asked for a ride to a telephone, or the nearest police station or mountain rescue centre. The astonished men said they would take him to Golden, BC, which was the closest place to contact anyone.

Luckily, on their way out they came upon a logging truck with a radio. Bland notified the RCMP in Golden of the accident in the hope of initiating a rescue. When he reached Golden, he contacted his commanding officer in Wainwright, Alberta, and the RCMP contacted the warden service in Jasper. By this point, it was noon on June 15.

Immediately, rescue leader Gerry Israelson and five wardens were put on standby. Because it was an avalanche accident, Sam and I were also put on standby. I immediately checked in with dispatch to get more details. Once I understood the nature and size of the accident, I had them notify the closest available dog team, Gord Peyto and Saxon in Golden. It's always wise to call in two dog teams to work an avalanche deposit, especially if you suspect there are victims.

I headed to the rescue room, where Gerry updated us. The weather conditions at the Columbia Icefield were poor, so flying was questionable, but a team of wardens was already at the staging area. The operation was coming together quickly. I headed for the staging area myself, arriving there about 2:30 p.m. My first priority was to gear up Sam with a tracking harness and avalanche transceiver—a precaution we all used when searching in a potentially hazardous avalanche situation.

There were 12 wardens at the staging area, waiting for the helicopter to arrive and the weather to lift. Gord wasn't there yet, but I wasn't worried. He knew this was an emergency and would be driving madly, siren blaring and lights flashing. We had enough staff to handle the search, and I was hopeful that the dogs would find the climbers quickly.

Corporal Bland arrived shortly after I did, and Gerry immediately took him aside to interview him. His story was as follows: On the afternoon of June 13, Bland and captains Willison, Wolf and Mavromatis set out from the parking lot at the Columbia Icefield for a series of planned climbs. That evening, they established a camp above the Athabasca Glacier's third icefall. Willison was the leader and the most experienced climber. Wolf and Mavromatis were also fairly experienced, but Bland, a late replacement for another officer, was only a novice climber.

At approximately 11:30 a.m. on June 14, the group headed out on foot for Mt. Columbia. The pace was slow as they left their camp. To the west stood Mt. Columbia, the highest point in Alberta at 3,747 metres. To the southwest was Mt. Bryce. Willison decided on the route the group would take. But unknown to Bland, they were not heading for Mt. Columbia, but the much more formidable Mt. Bryce.

As they reached the base of a long and substantial cliff, a break in the rock offered a good route to the ridge above. This was on the eastern flank of the mountain's northeastern ridge. The narrow gully of steep snow extended through the cliff band up to a funnel, or couloir. This allowed the four men to climb on steep snow rather than rock, simplifying the ascent of the funnel up and over its corniced rim.

At the base of the climb, Willison briefed everyone on how they would climb the funnel. They would proceed on two independent ropes, two to a rope. Willison and Bland were on a blue rope; Wolf and Mavromatis were on a red rope. Willison led, with Bland following. They climbed through the cliff band to the funnel, an open, convex slope of steep snow, between 40 and 50 degrees. Above this, a large cornice loomed over them. To avoid the cornice, the climbers headed left, to where the cornice petered out next to a rock buttress. Beyond that, they would be on a relatively flat ridge that ran toward the peak itself. Willison and Bland alternated leading the rope up the slope toward the lip, placing belay anchors as they went. Wolf and Mavromatis followed independently in the same fashion.

After climbing about 240 vertical metres, Bland reached a point next to the buttress and set up his belay anchor. He clipped in, got comfortable, then started to take up the rope as Willison climbed toward him. Bland could see the other pair below and off to one side. Without warning, the cornice at the top of the funnel broke, raining massive ice and snow chunks on the climbers. An avalanche was triggered. Bland tightened, waiting for Willison's weight to yank on the rope as the avalanche hit him. Bland felt a sharp jolt, and then the rope broke. He heard the freight-train roar of thundering snow as it exploded onto the terrain below. The entire couloir purged clean before his eyes, like a toilet bowl flushing. Miraculously, Bland remained seated as tonnes

An avalanche hits the Icefield Parkway in Banff National Park.

of snow spread out on the glacier below—by all accounts, he too should have been ripped out of his belay station and hurled down the mountain.

Now there was silence. A smooth sheet of ice remained where his fellow climbers once were. Disconnecting himself from his anchor, Bland edged down the rocks to a point where he could observe the avalanche area. He saw one person stirring on the surface, possibly Wolf or Willison. He called down and thought he got a response—then all was still.

Bland had to find a route down, but he could see

nothing. The snow slope they had climbed up was now denuded of snow, and the funnel was nothing more than smooth ice, resembling stainless steel. It would have been suicide to navigate down the way they had come up without protection from a rope and anchor. After half an hour of indecision, Bland decided to move up, sticking to the solid rock buttress. From there, he would be able to see what options presented themselves.

What he found was a gentle ridge that stretched toward the main mountain itself. Like the prow of a great ship, the rock stretched up another 730 metres to the summit. From there, he saw the distant river that would lead to his rescue.

As Bland recounted his adventure, adamant they'd been climbing Mt. Columbia, there was plenty of confusion. If that was the case, his journey down the backside of the mountain would have been of epic proportions. One look at the topographical map indicated how impossible this would have been given the precipitous drops and the trackless distance to the logging road. However, the rescue party had to take the corporal's word. So, at approximately 4:30 p.m., when the weather broke, Gerry, Warden Rick Ralf and Corporal Bland set off in the helicopter to do a reconnaissance of Mt. Columbia.

But as they approached the mountain, Bland became confused. He didn't recognize the terrain at all. There was no sign of a funnel, cliff band, avalanche deposit or steep, rocky buttresses on the upper half of the mountain. All he saw were the white slopes of Mt. Columbia's relatively smooth eastern approach.

Aware of Bland's escape route, Gerry thought the description fit the Mt. Bryce area, so he directed the search to that peak. As they approached, they saw a large avalanche deposit at the base of a long cliff, and Bland immediately recognized the area. For some reason unknown to Bland, they had climbed Mt. Bryce instead of Mt. Columbia. The three senior officers must have decided to change their route, but did not communicate the new objective to the more inexperienced corporal.

When Gerry announced over the radio that they had found the accident site, there was a bustle of activity around us. Gord had arrived with Saxon, and the dogs picked up on the change in atmosphere and started whining.

From the air, Gerry and Rick scanned the slide surface. One climber was lying on the snow surface. The helicopter landed approximately 200 metres away, downwind from the slide, and the wardens marked a safe route across the glacier to the slide deposit. A quick check of the victim, determined to be Wolf, revealed no signs of life.

At 5:20 p.m., I flew in with fellow warden Joe Buker, equipped with all the necessary gear for a night out. The avalanche deposit was enormous. On the front leading edge, near the deposit's southeastern corner, lay the one exposed body.

As I walked toward the deposit, I released Sam, who

quickly bounded ahead to the body. After giving him a minute to satisfy his curiosity, I took him away from the body and turned him loose to search. At first he was still distracted by the exposed victim, but he soon settled down to look for something under the snow. Rick carried a shovel, and Joe followed with a long probe. Both men had worked around Sam before and were careful not to crowd him. Sam was now fully focused on searching as he moved with agility over and around the large clumps of debris.

Because Wolf and Mavromatis had been roped together, I figured that Mavromatis should be somewhere near Wolf. This is where I concentrated Sam's initial search. Soon the dog started digging and had uncovered a jacket about eight metres up from the body by the time I reached him. I gave him a "Good boy" and got him working again.

By now, we'd been searching for more than an hour, and Sam had come up with nothing besides the jacket. I was getting concerned. We had covered at least a third of the deposit without any good indication. A dog handler's worst enemy—doubt—began simmering in my brain. Captain Mavromatis' body should have been in this sector. Had Sam missed the scent?

When Gord and Saxon arrived at the site, I moved Sam into the middle of the deposit. Shortly after they started searching, I heard Gord praise Saxon. Everyone looked up from what they were doing—even Sam, for he recognized a dog handler's praise. I figured Gord had found Mavromatis, but it turned out to be another red herring—this time a glove. No sooner had we got back to work than Sam started digging frantically. I raced toward him, waving to Joe and Rick to join us. Sam had winded something from about 30 metres away. By the time we got there, Sam had dug down to the body, which was about half a metre below the surface, and was tugging on the sleeve of a jacket.

Relieved, I praised Sam and moved him over to the far side of the avalanche deposit and back to work. Rick and Joe dug out the body. He was attached to a blue rope, so it had to be Willison, Bland's climbing partner. But Mavromatis' body refused to be found near his dead partner. Knowing Sam could have missed the scent if the body was deeply buried, Gord continued to search that area of the slide. Meanwhile, I continued where I was.

On a search, distractions are always a problem for working dogs, particularly helicopters, which usually mean exciting work is on hand for the dogs. As the helicopter arrived and departed, bringing in searchers and equipment, Sam and Saxon had ignored its noisy presence. But when it started flying directly over the deposit, it was another matter. On the last flight, an RCMP constable acting as coroner needed to take pictures of the deposit. The overhead flights were now hindering the dogs searching below. This was irksome, but after a few minutes of stopping and looking up, the dogs got back to work.

After 15 minutes, Sam uncovered a section of red

climbing rope, and I knew we were finally in the right area. He indicated the rope in two other spots before starting to dig about 20 metres away—he definitely had something. I waved Rick and Joe over, then pulled Sam off his digging while Joe probed around. On his second or third try, he hit an object. By the slight give in it, we knew it was either a pack or a body. Rick started shovelling and soon found Mavromatis' body, about a metre down. The red climbing rope attached to his body had snapped off a metre from his harness.

The search was over. Looking up, I saw the "hour-glass" shape of the terrain, with the funnel at the top and the deposit at the bottom. I saw the scar along the lip where the cornice had detached and the narrow chute the debris had funnelled through. It took a great force to break the climbing ropes and spit the men out onto opposite sides of a deposit as long as this. I solemnly reflected on the last minutes of the three men and how violent it must have been.

Later, I also reflected on the rescue team's response to the dogs. Since the first avalanche rescue involving a dog team, in 1972, much had been learned. With this avalanche search, I felt the dog program had matured into a well-functioning component of mountain search and rescue. The rescue personnel were well versed in the best use of search dogs and conducted themselves accordingly. It was reassuring to see how dedicated everyone was to the program. They now understood how to get the most out of a team—and it was to everyone's benefit.

Manhunt at Dead Man's Flats

DEAD MAN'S FLATS SPREADS OUT innocuously just inside the windy entrance to the Rocky Mountains, about 80 kilometres west of Calgary. Its colourful name comes from an equally colourful past—from either or both of two separate incidents. The first occurred between two brothers who operated a dairy farm on the flats. One brother apparently went insane and killed the other with an axe. The second incident involved two or three Native people trapping beaver illegally in Banff National Park, just after it was established. To avoid being caught by the park warden, they smeared beaver blood on themselves to "play dead." It worked. The warden ran for help and the men escaped.

The aptly named flats continued to attract crimes of passion. The area became the focus of a famous shootout in 1935 involving the RCMP's first dog team when Warden Bill Neish killed two fugitives running from the murder of two RCMP officers in Saskatchewan. Neish laconically reported to Ottawa, "Shot two bandits." When Ottawa asked for details, he followed up with a telegram reading, "Snowing like hell."

When Warden Scott Ward was called out to conduct a search at Dead Man's Flats in the spring of 1988, these old stories may have passed through his mind. Scott and his dog, Smokey, had been together only one year, but Smokey was a good tracking dog that took his time establishing the scent characteristics in a track. Once he locked onto it, he was hard to shake.

Each track has its own distinct scent, or scent picture. Much of the scent comes from cell-sized rafts of skin that continually slough off the body. These microscopic flakes carry the most distinct aspect of the scent's makeup. Other factors, such as a person's emotional state, also add to the picture. People often refer to the "fear scent" or "adrenalin rush"—pheromones released by the body that are detectable by a dog. RCMP dogs are trained to be "scent specific." That is, the dog picks up the freshest track available. This works well in rural areas, where there is little contamination from other people's tracks.

In this case, an older couple's motorhome had broken

down on the side of the Trans-Canada Highway. The couple was busy dealing with the problem when a car pulled up to investigate. Its occupants, two men and two women, were just passing by, but they were also looking for trouble. The couple thought the group had stopped to lend a hand, but soon found out otherwise. The passersby beat the couple and ransacked the motorhome, looking for valuables. The pensioners were left lying in the ditch while the thieves drove off in the motorhome. However, they got only a few kilometres down the road when the motorhome broke down again. Gathering up as many valuables as they could carry, the culprits took off into the bush on the north side of the highway.

When Scott arrived at 9:55 a.m., there were already a number of RCMP officers involved in the search. A helicopter being used for air reconnaissance soon spotted the abandoned motorhome, but there was no sign of the fugitives. Scott and Smokey were immediately teamed with two RCMP officers to accompany them on the track and act as backup. It took a while for Smokey to pick up the track, but soon they were off. They were only a few minutes into the track when Scott realized no one was following him—the officers were still back at the motorhome. Now Scott had to decide: return for his backup or keep going? He chose the latter.

Five more minutes into the track, Smokey stopped to investigate a hollow tree and came away with some clothing in his mouth. It belonged to the elderly couple and had been hastily stashed in the hollow of a dead tree. The track continued along the Bow River, then onto an access road, then back into the bush. Along the way, Smokey indicated more discarded clothing. Finally, after about 1.5 kilometres, they came out near the highway.

A hundred metres ahead, next to the busy highway, Scott saw the four suspects and yelled for them to stop. Taking one look at the warden and his dog, they fled across the highway. Once Scott gained the highway, he yelled again for them to stop. A man and woman stopped, but the other two continued running into the bush on the highway's south side. Scott radioed the RCMP that he had two of the suspects. After a few minutes, the other two walked out of the bush and gave themselves up peacefully.

Scott laid the suspects down prone on the meridian in the middle of the highway. It must have been quite a sight for passing motorists. Corporal Bill Hamilton, an RCMP dog handler from Calgary, arrived at about this time, as did the two backup RCMP officers, who took charge of the suspects. They searched the group but found no weapons or money.

However, according to the RCMP investigators at the crime scene, there was still more than $2,000 in cash missing that could have been stashed anywhere along the route. Scott, accompanied by Bill, used Smokey to backtrack the length of their passage through the bush. They reached the

Warden-service dog handlers with working dogs. From left to right: Scott Ward and Smokey, Dale Portman and Sam, and Gord Peyto and Saxon.

motorhome but had found nothing. Then Scott remembered that the two suspects had continued running into the bush before giving themselves up. Bill got his dog, Kelly, out of the truck and followed Scott over to the south side of the highway. Scott pointed out where he thought the two had entered the bush, and Bill put Kelly to work.

Within five minutes, Kelly found $2,100 in cash hidden under some moss.

It was a peaceful conclusion. Apart from a few bruises, the older couple had survived an unpleasant situation that could have been far worse. Thanks to the dogs, all their money and possessions were accounted for, and the suspects were apprehended without the expense of a large manhunt.

CHAPTER

9

Sam's Broken Leg

THE DAY STARTED WITH GREAT PROMISE—a blue sky, mild temperatures and an optimistic outlook. Sam and I had recently returned from our yearly recertification, where he'd done well. While training to apprehend criminals, he had even let go of his quarry when given the "Out" command. It was a command he often liked to ignore. So it was with confidence that I greeted him at his kennel one morning in January 1984. He sat there, eager as always, tail wagging with anticipation for what the day had to offer.

As we drove to the ski hill at Lake Louise, Sam paced in the back of my Suburban. I grabbed a coffee at the avalanche hut, said hello to the men working on avalanche control and loaded gear and Sam onto the snowmobile. We were on our way to train on a simulated avalanche exercise. Sam always rode in the open compartment behind the seat, next to my pack. As we drove up the Pika ski-out trail, he whined quietly, indicating his eagerness. Even though he always seemed to know whether we were off to a simulation or the real thing, he was always excited to get to work.

Soon we were out in the open, following a packed trail into Richardson Bowl, but the terrain steepened as we progressed, and we hit deep, untracked snow. The snowmobile started to bog down, so I decided to circle back and come at the slope again with more power.

As I came out of the turn to make another run at the hill, something killed the engine and locked the snowmobile's track, throwing me against the dashboard. I then heard a heart-stopping howl. I looked back and saw in horror that Sam's leg was jammed in the track. He was twisting violently in pain, trying to pull his leg free. He must have jumped off when I'd made the turn but, in trying to climb back on, had stepped on the slowly turning track with his back leg. It had been sucked into the machine.

I grasped Sam around the neck and tried to hold him still. He continued to howl and suddenly, with lightning speed, had my right hand in his mouth. I felt searing pain as his canines penetrated the mitts into my hand. I gave him a painful "No" as his eyes rolled back in his head. That didn't work, so I gave Sam the "Out" command, with no effect.

It might have worked on his recertification but not

under these circumstances. I was frantic. I was clamped to Sam and could not get to my radio in my pack. I had no way to call for help. As Sam thrashed his head about, I desperately tried to keep hold of his neck. If I lost my grip, there was a good chance he would relocate his teeth somewhere else on me.

Finally, after repeated commands of "Out," Sam slackened his grip, and I managed to rip my hand out of his mouth while still keeping a hold on his neck. My mind was racing, trying to figure out what to do, when a ski patroller stopped next to me—Sam's howling had brought him down. After explaining what happened, I asked the skier to get the leash out of my anorak pocket. Taking the leash, he overlapped two coils, making a sheepshank knot, and dropped it over Sam's muzzle. He tightened it around Sam's mouth and fastened the two ends at the back of his neck. Now that Sam was successfully muzzled, I could relax my grip and better assess the situation.

In a fortunate twist of fate, the skier turned out to be a veterinarian. He had drugs and a syringe in his pack. He gave Sam Demerol intravenously, and the dog soon calmed down. I got on the radio to call for additional help. Soon, we had a couple more ski patrollers there, as well as Gord Irwin, a park warden involved with Lake Louise's avalanche control program.

While the veterinarian held Sam, I got the idea that if I started the engine and put the machine in reverse, the leg would come free. My theory was to apply minimal pressure on the throttle. The track would slowly turn and Sam's leg would come around. But when I got thrown, my hip had hit the dashboard and bent the key flat—now it couldn't be turned.

As it turned out, this was lucky for Sam. His leg was so entwined in the track that had it turned in any direction it would have torn off. I called for a helicopter, ready to pay any costs to help my dog.

I returned my attention to Sam, soothing him with my voice while Gord worked to drop the snowmobile track. It took some time, but he was finally able to release the tension on the track and free Sam's leg. The vet assessed the damage and said it wasn't good. The thick bone in the leg's middle section was shattered. Fortunately, there was no blood, even though the wound was open and we could see shattered bones under the torn flesh. We immobilized the leg as best we could, then waited for the helicopter. The Demerol had done its job—Sam was surprisingly calm. His eyes followed every move we made, knowing it was all for his benefit. They always come to rest on me, though, seeking assurance as I stroked his head.

The vet advised me where to take Sam when we got to Calgary, and I thanked him for all his help. I don't know what I would have done without him. He then drew attention to my hand, which I'd forgotten about. Taking the mitt off, I saw that my hand had been ripped open in the fleshy part, between my thumb and forefinger. Like Sam's leg, there was no blood, just a gaping blue wound. One of the ski patrollers applied a couple of butterfly Band-Aids to close it, then covered it with a bandage. In the distance, we could hear the drone of a helicopter coming up the valley.

We carried Sam to the helicopter on a blanket, and I climbed in after him. I was so concerned about Sam that I don't remember much of the trip until the pilot mentioned we were nearing Calgary. He also notified me that someone from the Calgary City Police would meet us there. It was comforting to get all this attention for Sam. Search and rescue dogs are priceless when you consider their training and the results they achieve in the field. Who knew? Maybe Sam would repay one of Calgary's finest someday. Once we landed, we moved Sam carefully into the back of the police cruiser and headed for the North Hill Veterinary Clinic.

They were expecting us. A vet examined Sam right away, mumbling a lot and shaking his head. He eventually asked me to leave the room. I woodenly walked out, hoping he wouldn't put Sam down without my permission. As I sat in the waiting room, doubt spread through me. Finally, the vet came out to the reception desk. I could tell that things weren't good. He said, "That leg's probably going to have to come off."

I felt like my world was crumbling. All I could think about was poor Sam hopping around on three legs, so much potential gone—just like that. I blurted out, "He's a working

dog. We've got to give him a chance. Money's not an issue."
I was prepared to foot the bill myself if Parks Canada had
reservations. The vet looked at my hand. "You go get that
hand looked after and we'll see what we can do," he said. I
emphasized that nothing drastic should be done while I was
gone. He agreed.

The Foothills Hospital emergency ward was surprisingly
quiet. Before I knew it, I was in an examining room. While
I tried to remain stoic, the nurse washed and scrubbed the
wound with great zest using a bristled brush. I was hoping
for a soft cloth. When they spread the 6-centimetre wound,
I could see the tendons. As I explained to the doctor what
had happened, he told me how he had stitched up victims
of police-dog attacks and asked how it felt to have the shoe
on the other foot. He then waited about two seconds after
freezing the wound before he stitched me up. The wound
took 13 stitches.

The constable and I returned to the clinic. The prognosis
still wasn't good, but they were committed to trying to save
Sam's leg. They operated on him that afternoon. The next
morning, I arrived at the clinic promptly at 9:00 a.m. and
met with a vet who had helped with the operation. She said
that everything had gone well and that Sam was eager to go
home. He had a steel rod sticking out of the top of the cast
that ran the length of the large bone, and all the loose bone
slivers and pieces were wired to it.

The news that Sam could go home was encouraging, but

Kathy Calvert's CARDA-trained avalanche dog, Bear (left), and Sam.

there were three concerns: one was infection, the second was whether the leg would heal properly, and the third was that the injury not be disturbed in any way. It had to mend properly to adequately support his weight and the strenuous activity that goes with being a working dog. All I could do was follow instructions and hope. All Sam wanted to do was get in the truck, his security blanket.

Sam was on antibiotics for a month, during which time

he stayed in his kennel and was kept very quiet. For the next two months, I slowly increased his exercise regime until his cast came off. That was a big day for both of us. It was reassuring to see him put weight on the leg. All his walks were on a leash. That way, if a deer popped up or another dog appeared unannounced, Sam didn't have a chance to take off.

After a month, I started taking Sam out on walks with a longer leash, so he could range about. He could sniff a tree or bush while cocking his leg, letting the dogs and coyotes in the neighbourhood know that he was back. I stretched and massaged his leg, working it back and forth while he watched me with amusement.

One day, about four months after the accident, Sam went for a run. It wasn't a long run, but it did include short bursts of speed and quick changes in direction. When he was finished, I gave him the hand signal to come. Without hesitation, he was sitting in front of me, tail wagging and ears perked forward. I slapped my left thigh with my hand and with a jump he circled my right leg and came to a reasonable sit in the heel position. He tilted his head and looked up at me as if to say, "I'm back."

Sam was so eager that when the day came to get back on a snowmobile, he didn't hesitate. We drove off to another avalanche exercise while he sat on the seat in front of me, where I could keep an eye on him, barking his approval to one and all as we headed up the mountain.

Sam's Broken Leg

Sam and I worked well together as a team for another six rewarding years, until 1990. When he was nine years old and too old and stiff to work, he just hung around, spending his retirement on a sofa or going for peaceful walks. He looked amused the day I brought home Cody, another eager working dog. I'm sure Sam passed on his experiences to Cody—the warning about snowmobiles sure stuck, for Cody was never comfortable travelling on them.

10

Off the Beaten Path

BANFF NATIONAL PARK IS KNOWN for its majestic peaks with imposing rock faces that tower over scenic valleys. The Spray Valley separates Mt. Rundle to the east from Sulphur Mountain to the west. The town of Banff, nestled at the foot of wedge-shaped Mt. Rundle, provides a perfect setting for spectacle-seeking visitors. Like a Bavarian castle, the famous Banff Springs Hotel presides over the panoramic view. Nearby, in the shadow of Sulphur Mountain, lie the equally popular, mineral-rich hot springs.

Sulphur Mountain lacks the spectacular form of its taller neighbour, Rundle. Dark timber infringes on its modest, curved summit that reaches only 2,440 metres. However, Sulphur is one of the most conquered summits in the Canadian Rockies—mainly because a gondola takes people to its top. There's a place to dine and a souvenir shop, as well as accessible views of the spectacular surrounding landscape. The Bow and Spray valleys meet at the Banff Springs Hotel and the green links of its golf course spread out far below.

An established trail switchbacks up the mountain under the gondola route. People taking the gondola up might choose to walk down for the exercise, happy for an opportunity to stretch their legs in the mountain environment. Others who want a more vigorous outing might walk up the trail and take the gondola down.

On March 6, 1989, one young man chose a slightly different option. One of hundreds of Canadians who migrate annually to work and play in Banff National Park, Brian was eager to climb this mountain behind the Banff Springs Hotel, where he worked.

Although this was his first trip out west, and he'd only been in the mountains for three weeks, Brian was already behaving like a local. He considered the gondola trip up Sulphur reserved for the "gorbies"—the locals' nickname for tourists. When even the hiking trail did not provide enough challenge, Brian opted to search for his own route up. His plan was to gain the ridge—which appeared attainable even for a rookie climber—then walk casually up to the summit. He intended to catch a gondola ride down in plenty of time to soak in the springs before sampling Banff's vibrant nightlife.

He began his day bushwhacking up through the trees near the Upper Hot Springs facility, snaking around the many obstacles. Thick undergrowth, deadfall and small rock outcroppings occasionally blocked his path and slowed his progress. The terrain gradually became steeper until he started to encounter small cliff bands and pitches of slab rock. But as he got higher on the mountain, the bands of rock and slab pitches slowly fused together into one solid cliff that magnified the challenge. Only a few thin game trails intersected his path. Even the sure-footed deer did not try to go straight up this mountain.

Brian soon found himself pushing past his skill level and limited experience. Ironically, the terrain made it easier for him to continue up than turn back down. Finally, he reached the crux. He slipped, sliding down the rock a good distance, and came to rest awkwardly on his foot. Scraped and bruised, he worried about the sharp pain coming from his ankle. But he was also getting desperate to reach the top and the gondola ride home.

The sun had moved over the mountain's crest in its westward journey. In the cool shade, Brian was starting to shiver. Fortunately, adrenalin kept his bad ankle working, despite the pain. He lurched onward, knowing time was running out for both daylight and his mobility. Reattempting the ridge, he slipped and fell again. This time he landed in a dark gully, still choked with the winter's snow. The snow cushioned his fall but also soaked his lightweight clothes.

No longer able to bear weight, his ankle had now failed him completely. His plan to get to the top before the gondola shut down for the night seemed impossible. Escaping the gully and the snow's formidable cold became his more immediate concern. Dragging himself with his arms through the waist-deep snow, he trailed his injured limb. He finally struggled to a small level spot on a rock ledge where he could ponder his situation.

Brian felt encouraged getting out of the snow, but only for a moment. When he started that day, he had never considered spending the night out. Panic now took hold as he realized how badly his ankle was swelling. Despite the exhausting activity, Brian's body temperature was beginning to drop dangerously. Because he was stranded far from the hiking trail or shelter, unable to move, he knew he risked exposure.

Brian could think of nothing else to do but call for help. Yelling until he was hoarse, he received no reply. Since he could barely see the miniature Banff Springs Hotel, or the outsized parking lot between the Sulphur Mountain gondola terminal and the Upper Hot Springs, this came as no surprise.

Amazingly, staff at the hot springs *had* heard his muffled calls, but dismissed them as kids fooling around. One woman out for a walk, however, reported what she thought might be cries for help to the Parks Canada Warden Service. Although such reports often turn out to be false alarms, a call was put through to Scott Ward, a park warden and the local dog handler. Even with little to go on, Scott was obliged to check it out.

When he got to the hot springs, he interviewed the staff members who said they had heard the faint calls. There had been no response, they said, when they tried yelling back. Away from the noisy pool, and closer to the parking lot, Scott also tried yelling but got no result.

Not knowing what else to do, Scott got his dog, Smokey, out of the truck and put him in his tracking harness. Casting about behind the hot springs, they tried to pick up a fresh track for the dog to work. Since visitors traipsed around the springs every day, Scott expected tracks to go only a short distance then return to some other point near the facility. If nothing else came of their search, he figured, at least the outing would serve as a bit of training for the dog.

Parks Canada canines, trained at the RCMP dog-training facility near Innisfail, Alberta, are taught to take the freshest or first track encountered. Once a dog locks onto a certain track, he is supposed to stay with it. Some breeds, like bloodhounds, are given an article of clothing so they will pursue only that particular scent. Both methods have advantages and disadvantages. Since there was no article of clothing to give to the dog this day, Smokey's training fit the bill.

After casting about for a while, the dog finally picked up a track, and Scott let him run with it. Soon they were snaking up through the trees. The track could have belonged to any hiker, so at first Scott wasn't as excited as Smokey. It might have connected with a trail that would lead them off in the wrong direction. To Scott's surprise, the track continued to move off-trail and uphill—in the direction of the reported cries.

While the climbing was easy for the determined dog, it was hard work for Scott. In some places, he had to set the dog down for a rest while he caught his breath. In other places, he had to drop the tracking line and catch up. The delays were only temporary, though, and the two continued relentlessly upward. Scott was a fit long-distance runner, but even he couldn't compete with an eager dog on a steep, uphill track. Scott now realized they were tracking someone who wasn't following an orthodox trail to the summit.

The pair climbed steadily through the bush and timber as the terrain became progressively steeper. Not only was Smokey a very good tracking dog, but his agility was also first class. In a couple of places, though, even the eager dog lost his grip and slid back down, only to catch himself and continue.

Smokey then made a dramatic switch in his behavior. He focused on a spot at the base of a steep cliff. The dog investigated the scene in canine fashion, trying to figure out what had happened. Scott knew to let the dog finish his examination. Although he had confidence in Smokey and his finely tuned nose, he was also reassured by a fresh boot track in the soft dirt approaching the cliff. He had no doubt

Park warden Scott Ward with his service dog Dana.

they were on someone's trail, but it was up to the dog now to solve the puzzle and find their quarry—dead or alive.

Smokey peered up the cliff for a short time, then moved on farther to the left, skirting the base of another cliff. He stopped in several places to sniff at overturned rocks and disturbed vegetation. The dog was putting the pieces together, forming a picture. Finally, he started to work his way along the base, trying to find another trace of the track.

All of a sudden, Smokey went off with renewed vigour toward a gully plugged with snow. The dog's head swung like a swivel on a hinge. Looking up the mountain, he dropped to his belly and started clawing his way up the steep terrain again, more determined than ever. Following all of this with great interest, Scott saw where the dog was headed. Ten metres above them, he spotted what looked like a man's shape huddled on a ledge.

Earlier, frozen and exhausted, Brian had given up shouting. He resigned himself to the fact that it might be a day or two before someone might start looking for him—if and when his supervisor at the hotel reported him missing. By then, he knew it might be too late.

Instead, sporting a yellow harness and dragging his 25-foot tracking line, a canine rescuer now stood proudly looking up at him. Smokey glanced backward briefly, as if wondering, "What's taking Scott so long?" Waiting for instruction, the vigilant dog refocused on his astonished quarry. Smokey made no move toward Brian, for he had also been trained to track fugitives. If his quarry was to flee, he was ready to drag him down.

When his heavy-breathing handler finally joined him, Smokey acknowledged him without moving his head but with a slight tremble of anticipation. Scott petted and praised the dog vigorously, "Good boy, good boy, Smokey." The dog's ears went down for a moment and his tail moved back and forth, for he knew his job was done. The rest was up to Scott.

After Scott immobilized Brian's swollen and discoloured ankle, he pulled out his radio to request a helicopter from the Banff warden service. With dusk approaching, Scott asked for a sling harness for himself and a special harness for the dog. Fortunately, they were in an open space on the mountain where a helicopter could reach them with a long line.

A half hour later, they could hear the single-engine Bell 206 Jet Ranger coming up the valley. A park warden in bright orange coveralls hung underneath on a 60-foot sling rope. A minute later, the warden was kneeling next to them with a first-aid kit and a Jenny Bag. Placing Brian in the bag with only his nose sticking out, the warden sat next to his patient in a sling and prepared to evacuate.

Twenty minutes later, the helicopter returned for Scott and Smokey. Scott knew everything needed to go smoothly when slinging the dog. If Smokey was to have a traumatic experience, his confidence in the system might never be restored. Scott reviewed his checklist, making sure Smokey was properly set up in his harness and all the carabiners were connected. Then, he just had to hope for the best.

The helicopter lifted the pair off the ground slowly and carefully. Once in the air, Smokey tucked his tail under his body and looked around curiously. As the helicopter started moving horizontally, its airspeed picked up and suddenly the two passengers were swung around with their backs to the wind. The dog tucked his head under Scott's arm so his handler could serve as a barrier to the rushing air. Scott gave the dog a much-appreciated scratch behind the ear.

When the Banff warden office came into view and the helicopter's speed decreased, Smokey pulled his head out from under Scott's arm. His ears came forward as he again became enthralled with the view. Even though he seemed to be enjoying the ride, Smokey was anxious to land. Not only was it well past dinnertime, but no water had been available on the mountain. When the helicopter landed, the hard-working dog headed straight for a galvanized pail to get a cool drink of water.

In Canada's mountain parks, skeletal remains of lost or injured visitors are occasionally found. Smokey rescued one lucky adventurer from such a fate that day—and certainly earned his water and more.

CHAPTER

11

The Healy Creek
Avalanche

BY THE END OF THE 1980S, park wardens working in search and rescue had seen many different types of rescue situations. In 1990, as the decade dawned, their search procedures would be put to the test in the biggest avalanche recovery effort up to that time. The Healy Creek avalanche created conditions that rescuers had never encountered before, and it became a benchmark in their understanding of avalanche rescue.

The accident occurred on Sunday, February 11, 1990, on the trail to Healy Pass, a popular ski route that begins at the Sunshine ski area parking lot. Five older, experienced skiers set out for the day, intending to get as far up the trail as they felt comfortable with, given the poor weather and deep snow. They were following a broken trail forged by two independent parties a couple of hours ahead of them, which made it easier to keep going.

Despite the broken trail, the skiers were slow because of difficulty with their choice of ski wax due to the wet snow and warm temperatures. One party member, tired from a previous day's outing, was having difficulty keeping up with the others. However, she wasn't worried when she lost sight of the rest of the party part of the way up the trail. She continued at her own pace but was startled by a deep rumbling farther up the valley. It was approximately 12:15 p.m. Possibly because of fatigue, she turned back at this point and headed for the parking lot. On the way, she ran into another party of two and asked them to keep an eye out for her four friends.

The two skiers continued on, despite having also heard the rumblings. Within a short time, they found the cause of the ominous noise. The fresh ski tracks they were following led straight into a huge avalanche deposit that had obliterated the trail. There was no doubt that the avalanche had just come down—the overwhelming smell of spruce balm, freshly smashed trees and shattered debris told them that. Even so, it had already set as hard as concrete. After they crossed the avalanche deposit, they noticed older ski tracks emerging from the other side covered with newly fallen snow, distinct from the tracks they were following. The pair continued up the trail until they encountered the first pair returning. The skiers all became alarmed when it was established that the returning pair hadn't seen the missing group of four. They discussed the matter briefly, then all turned back to investigate the avalanche. When they reached the monstrous slide, they did a hasty search but saw no sign of the missing skiers. They felt something was drastically wrong, however, and skied out to the parking lot with all possible haste to inform the employees at the Sunshine ticket wicket. The alarm was passed immediately to the warden service, who had been receiving reports of avalanches all day.

Tim Auger took this latest news very seriously and initiated a full-scale search at 4:30 p.m. Mark Ledwidge, working at the ski hill, left for the parking lot immediately to talk to the reporting individuals. There he met Tim as well as Scott Ward with Smokey. Clair Israelson was notified in Lake Louise and calls went out to put rescue personnel in other parks on standby. While other wardens continued to arrive, Tim and Scott took advantage of what visibility was still available to fly the valley looking for signs of the missing party. All they saw was what looked like a huge avalanche across the trail and two heavily laden skiers who did not fit the description of the people they were looking for.

The size of the slide was discouraging, but they had to proceed as though people were still alive. Mark Ledwidge and Peter Enderwick headed in with snowmobiles, which proved to be a daunting task, but they needed a broken trail to bring in rescue workers when the helicopter could no longer fly. Before the light failed completely, searchers were flown to the deposit and began probing areas where natural traps might pin a body. The surface was searched for any articles that may have been overlooked, but nothing was found. By dark, the ground search was called off, and everyone headed back to the warden office for a debriefing and to develop a contingency plan for the next day. Meanwhile, many things had been taken care of: personnel had been assigned to various tasks, such as supplies and equipment, liaising and dispatch and organization of volunteers, and a camp coordinator had been assigned.

The Banff dog team, Scott Ward and Smokey, were the first to search the deposit during the afternoon and early evening on the day of the accident. They were soon joined by the Glacier/Revelstoke team, Gord Peyto and Baron. They covered as much of the open deposit as they could in the time they had before nightfall, but also found nothing. This was unusual when it supposedly involved four people.

The next day, I joined Peyto and Ward with my new dog, Cody. An RCMP team from Cranbrook, BC, and Gord Burns and his young dog, Griz, also arrived. During the early hours of the second day, the temperature dropped dramatically to -30°C. When the searchers went back the following morning, they finally got a good look at the enormity of the slide. Two days prior to the accident, nearly 70 centimetres of snow had fallen in the area at temperatures

Cody rests after a lengthy search at the Healy Creek avalanche.

near or just below freezing. The avalanche deposit was 185 metres wide where it crossed the ski trail, making the new avalanche path 67 metres wider than it had been before the giant slide came down. Consequently, it had taken out many of the large Engelmann spruce that defined the old path. Trees were snapped off and branches up to 10 metres up the tree trunks were stripped clean. It all extended down into Healy Creek itself and cleared a swath 70 metres up the other side of the valley.

94

The open areas of the deposit were split into search units where probe teams worked alongside the search dogs. The avalanche debris was very hard as a result of the cold temperatures. Scent starts to freeze at around -20°C, so the dogs experienced very little or no scent coming to the surface. The dog teams were rotated throughout the day, working for two-hour stretches, then warming up and resting in the large, wood-heated tent that was set up on the edge of the deposit. Again and again, the dogs came up with nothing, and frustration was beginning to set in.

The weather change had also brought clear skies, and Tim was able to fly once again to check to see if by some remote chance the skiers might have wandered off the trail and become lost in the storm. He was also able to see what had caused the avalanche and to check the first path to see if further stabilization was necessary for the safety of the rescue workers.

By the end of the day, there was not even a hint of the skiers in the debris. At the evening's debriefing, everyone was registering frustration, particularly the dog handlers. No one had ever been on a slide worked so consistently by so many people with absolutely no results. Tim was heard to say, "It is almost inconceivable for four people to disappear without a trace," but on seeing the avalanche, we quickly recognized that possibility. The warden service upgraded the search and brought in wardens from other parks, as well as park rangers from nearby Kananaskis Country. As soon as a person was brought to the site, he or she was assigned a group and a location to search.

Early the next morning, Tim had the slide path bombed to eliminate any threat of secondary avalanches. It was a good call. The avalanche that was released swept down over the trail and wiped out the helicopter landing pad. This was quickly re-established, as was a large camp close to the search area but far enough away that it would not contribute any scent contamination. There was a propane-heated tent for the repeatedly returning workers as well as a second wood-heated wall tent for hot food and drinks. In those temperatures, the tents were used frequently, and only two people developed any frostbite. On the morning of the third day, at temperatures of -33°C, the four dog teams and probe lines commenced searching again.

With no surface articles to indicate where people might be buried, the rescuers began to wonder whether they were searching the right area. After thoroughly searching the open areas assigned to him, RCMP officer Gord Burns and Griz reluctantly moved on to search the treed area west of the slide path. It was extensively covered with broken tree branches that released a strong evergreen scent that was noticeable to the handlers. These broken branches were well mixed into the snow, making it difficult for Griz to work.

But dogs often amaze their handlers, and at about 9:30 a.m., Griz indicated the tip of a ski just under the snow and then indicated something buried farther down.

The probers quickly confirmed the presence of a body two metres down, but it took considerable time to shovel down to the victim. At last the dogs were finding something, despite the appalling conditions. Gord continued searching in the trees and succeeded in turning up several articles of clothing and a pack. With the discovery of the first body and these articles, the searchmaster realized the trees had to be the prime search area. Everyone also began to realize that probing the area seemed to help the dogs by allowing the scent to reach the surface more easily. With Gord covering the trees, the other three dog teams remained working the main deposit, as it could not yet be eliminated.

At about 3 p.m., one of the probe lines located the second victim at about the same depth, also in the trees. Steel shovels had to be used to dig down to the victim. By the end of the day, the entire area in the trees had been coarsely probed, with some areas being finely probed. The next day saw a renewal of activity in the treed area, and all the dogs concentrated their efforts there.

The media finally had something to report. Perry Jacobson and Keith Everts, both assistant chief park wardens, were the liaison officers for the media and family—a job not envied by anyone, but for which they were highly praised. They showed discretion, tact and compassion, particularly to family members. Two families went home with some closure, but two more bodies still remained to be found, and the snow gave them up reluctantly. At the end of the third day, the remaining victims still remained entombed in frozen silence, but at least the search area was now confined to the thickest part of the trees. The party had not been hit in the open on the avalanche path but had been well into the apparent safety of the trees.

The dog work on the final day was aided by the holes punched into the icy crust from the previous day's probing, which had allowed the scent to reach the surface. It was still difficult for the dogs, as they had to maintain a tight search pattern and keep their noses close to the surface of the snow. Even though Griz was fortunate enough to be in the right area for success, the stamina of all the dogs was tested fully over the four days of the search. By midmorning on the fourth day, Griz once again validated his master's faith in him. Now they began finding more articles of clothing. When the sun's rays finally warmed up the air slightly, Griz enthusiastically indicated in another area of the timbered deposit, and the two remaining victims were found together under a log. The probe lines had covered this area the previous day without luck.

Now, the course of events started to become clear. The friends had crossed the slide path and were probably intending to return to the parking lot after having their lunch around noon. They had moved well into the stand of old, massive trees, where they must have felt safe. Some of the trees were so big it would take two people to encircle them, indicating no evidence of slide activity for many years. Evidence of food in the victims' mouths indicated they were eating when the slide hit. The slide was released when one of the large cornices on the ridge above the valley broke off and hit the wind-loaded slope below. The resultant slide was so massive that the wind blast alone would have hurtled them into the surrounding forest. The trees that were expected to provide safety had been stripped of branches from the wind blast. The impact was sudden and complete. The skiers may have heard the immediate sound of the exploding avalanche as it plunged downward with a fearsome velocity and may have even looked toward the slide path expecting to see it go by. Nothing prepared them for the huge slide that mowed down the protective ancient forest where they ate their last meal.

In the end, the rescue workers concluded that the skiers had done everything they could have done except stay home. Risk-management reports completed after the incident pointed out that they were not wearing avalanche beacons, but that beacons would not have saved them. They would, however, have expedited the search and made it less risky for the many searchers exposed to a possible avalanche from the first slide path. The reports also carried a strong recommendation that people continue to use beacons and pointed out areas of improvement for future searches. Although no search is perfect, it was undeniable that the warden service had reached new heights of aptitude in handling large and complex rescue scenarios involving

Searchers dig out victims at the site of the Healy Creek avalanche.

multi-agency cooperation. Egos had been left at the office doors and tent flaps, giving Kevin Blades, in an article for *Viewpoint* magazine, a reason to compliment all involved for their professionalism.

It was not only the human searchers who performed well. The large, wet avalanche deposit that froze at -30°C and turned to concrete made it very difficult for the dogs to work. It went from being a large-article search, looking for a body in the snow, to a small-article search, like looking for the dime that Ginger found in the avalanche deposit on Mt. Edith Cavell. The dogs had to search more slowly and incorporate a much tighter search grid, which meant it took a long time to cover a designated area. Because of how thoroughly the dogs had to search, they had to be rested much more often and needed much more stamina. Once the dog teams at Healy Creek understood this, the dogs adapted well and achieved good results.

CHAPTER

12

Keno

"THE FIRST WORKING DOG THAT recovers a live person from an avalanche [in Canada] will be one that is either working at a ski resort or located there temporarily for training purposes. No professional team will be able to respond in time," said Corporal Gord Burns, an RCMP dog handler whose dog was also trained for avalanche recovery. Corporal Burns was referring to the fact that most rescue-dog teams are rarely located close enough to an avalanche accident to respond in time. A person caught and buried in an avalanche for up to 30 minutes has a reasonable chance of survival, after that the rate drops dramatically. Unless there is a large air space around the head, suffocation comes quickly. Even then, hypothermia is always another factor that hampers live recovery. The secret to a successful recovery is a quick detection of under 30 minutes.

When he made his comments, Burns was addressing a number of trainees at a Canadian Avalanche Rescue Dog Association (CARDA) course in 1984 at Island Lake Lodge, close to the Fernie Alpine Resort in the southeastern corner of BC. He was instructing an assortment of volunteers and ski-hill personnel who were there to train their dogs in avalanche search and rescue. Gord believed that it was particularly important for ski areas to invest in avalanche-dog teams. Skiers in resort areas usually are not familiar with backcountry travel and as a rule do not carry avalanche beacons and other equipment that aid in victim location. First responders are often survivors of the accident, and avalanche probes may be the only method available to them for locating victims, apart from skis or poles. If the victims are not located near the surface, shovels are needed as well.

This is a slow process and not likely to yield a positive result except by chance or if an article is found on the surface that would narrow down the search area. Before CARDA was established, the only avalanche-dog teams in the country were the RCMP and park wardens in our national parks. There were only a handful scattered throughout BC and Alberta, and, except for teams in Banff and Jasper national parks, none were located close to a ski area or any major backcountry ski facility. As it turned out, Burns' observation would prove prophetic.

Robin Siggers was enjoying a sunny day on the Fernie ski hill, doing a job he felt fortunate to have. He was the lead ski patroller at Fernie and found the work challenging and very rewarding, for he loved to ski. He was also one of three handlers with a trained avalanche rescue dog at the resort. This aspect of the job often took up a big part of his day, but since dogs are a full-time commitment, his dedication to the job went far beyond work hours. Every day, Robin and Keno would arrive at the hill, whether it was a training day or not. When Robin was engaged in other duties, Keno would stay in his kennel at the base of the ski hill, available if needed on a rescue.

Keno was a five-year-old golden lab/border-collie cross that earned his full CARDA certification when he was two years old. His training standard was maintained by yearly refresher courses with CARDA and, of course, frequent training days with the other teams at the hill. Still, as Burns also liked to mention, a training scenario is not the real thing. No matter how realistic the scenarios may be, there is no substitute for the pressure of an actual rescue. One of the main problems for volunteer dog handlers back then was that they rarely attended the real thing. This was sometimes because of their location, but also because professional teams were usually called in first, and the volunteers were not accepted as legitimate by some professional handlers.

The adrenalin level and excitement at a search when a

person's life is at stake cannot be duplicated—and dogs are very sensitive to this atmosphere. They pick up on any nervousness or excitement the handler or those around him exude. This can prove intimidating or even too exciting for the dogs and might interfere with their ability to settle down and work. Robin and Keno had yet to face this test, and every training session reminded Robin of that.

On December 20, 2000, the members of the ski patrol were concerned about having the hill ready for the early Christmas crowds. They wanted to open the entire hill to the public but needed to be utterly sure the slopes were safe. The early season is often the busiest period for staff preparing the slopes, as the snow is still new and has not yet built up the deep, stable snowpack that later snowfalls usually bring. As the season progresses, skier activity adds to the stability of the slopes.

On this day, they were particularly worried about deep-slab instability on the snow-laden upper slopes above Shakey's Acres ski run, on the left side of the White Pass quad chairlift. Previous bombing efforts had failed to release the snow, but they felt it was still hanging there above, ready to flood the slopes below if given the right trigger. To be safe, they decided to close the area until they got the required results with further bombing. The lift operator running the White Pass chairlift that day was a 21-year-old man named Ryan Radchenko. Ryan was well known in the area, having spent part of the previous summer working with Robin doing carpentry work at the ski hill. At the time, he jokingly observed that he was getting to know Keno, thinking this would give him an advantage if the dog ever had to look for him in an avalanche. Keno would certainly look for him, but not through familiarity, as avalanche dogs respond equally to any human scent associated with a buried body.

Radchenko, like all ski-hill employees, had taken the obligatory avalanche awareness training conducted by the ski patrol. Robin felt everyone was at risk when working in avalanche-prone country, and the best precaution was prevention through training. All staff were fully briefed on safe zones and escape routes to be used when the hazard was high, as well as the correct action to take if they were caught in an avalanche. Ryan retained the information on what to do when caught in a slide, but hadn't understood where or where not to be during closures.

In the early afternoon, during Ryan's lunch break, two patrollers set out to place closure signs on the Shakey's Acres ski run and all the other runs to the left of the White Pass chairlift. The two men had traversed a short way above the run to add additional signs after having placed closure signs near the lift terminus. They had no desire to be accused of not properly closing the area because of poor signage. Once the area was closed and clear of any skiers, they could continue working on stabilizing the threatening, wind-loaded slopes above.

Before moving on, they took a last look at Shakey's Acres.

To their astonishment, when they looked down the run they saw a lone skier not five metres below them. Gesticulating, they realized it was Ryan Radchenko and immediately yelled for him to get back to the lift. They barely managed to shout, "Area closed, get back!" when the large slab they had been worried about released under the added weight of the skier. Shocked, they watched as the man was overwhelmed by the rushing snow. They tried valiantly to spot the body now rapidly disappearing beneath the churning slabs. Once the slide came to a halt and there was no evidence of Ryan anywhere on the surface of the debris, they called out on their radios. The alarm went out immediately to other patrollers, and in particular to Robin, who was working on another part of the hill.

No doubt the patrollers were wondering, "How could this have happened? Didn't he see the 'Area Closed' signs?" The fact was that he had missed the closure announcement. Ryan's job as a lift operator gave him free skiing on work breaks or days off. And what young man doesn't appreciate the perks of working at a winter ski resort? He often used his lunch break to get in as many runs as he could, but this proved dangerous on that sunny December day. Ryan was riding the lift when the announcement was sent out to all employees that the Shakey's Acres ski run would be closed for avalanche control. He was unprepared for the closure when he stepped off the lift. Suddenly, he spotted the two patrollers traversing above him to his left. Seeing

Avalanche search dogs are trained near Oberstaufen, Bavaria, with the German Bergwacht.

people on skis in any area, particularly when they appear to be experienced personnel, often leads to a false sense of safety and may have led him to question the seriousness of the closure signs. Ryan may have even have thought that, as an employee, the closure did not apply to him—after all, he knew the patrollers individually as friends, and if they were there it must be safe. He was startled at their reaction to his presence as he skied onto the slope just below them, but their yells left no doubt that he should leave. It was too late. The thick layers of condensed, wind-packed snow abruptly released in one mass above him.

Galvanized by the sight of a wall of snow rushing at him like a tidal wave, Ryan mentally reviewed what he had been taught about surviving an avalanche. He remembered everything in nanoseconds. Swim with the snow to remain on top. If buried, make an air pocket around the mouth. Thrust your hand up toward the surface if you can still tell what direction is up.

Ryan desperately tried to remain calm as he attempted to keep his head above the tumbling, broken slabs of snow, but when it settled around him, he thought he was going to die. He was also aware that he was not wearing a transceiver, which would have helped the patrollers find him. He wanted to avoid panic in order to preserve his limited oxygen supply, but the air soon toxified into carbon monoxide, and he slid into unconsciousness. He would know nothing of the frantic search efforts that were taking place on the surface, nor would he be conscious to greet his ultimate rescuer.

Robin knew the minute he got the call that he and Keno would never reach the slide before critical survival time began to run out. But even if he thought this would only be a body recovery, it was still the real situation, and all his training with Keno would now be on the line. To reach the avalanche, he would have to ski to the bottom of the White Pass chairlift, ride the eight minutes lift to the top, collect his dog and ski down to the avalanche site. He was radioing for someone to bring Keno up by snowmobile as he began one of the fastest descents he would make on a ski run. He reached the lift in record time, hoping there would be no unforeseen lift stoppages or slowdowns on the way up. As he was riding up, mentally absorbing what had happened, he saw several patrollers already working on the slide deposit across the way. He was not encouraged when he realized how big the deposit was. It was significant, with a run-out of 150 to 200 metres and was 7 metres thick at the deepest point. He could only hope that Ryan was near the surface.

Robin reached the site before Keno, who was still five minutes behind in the snowmobile. It gave him time to question what had happened, determine the last-seen point and where the rescuers had already searched, and decide where best to deploy the dog. Keno, meanwhile, had picked up the elevated excitement the minute he got on the snowmobile. The machine had barely come to a stop at the site when the dog leaped out, anxious to reach Robin and eager to work. He immediately plunged ahead of the probe line to investigate the surface for any telltale scent. Keno was so quick, Robin was not immediately sure where the dog had found the glove that he suddenly presented to Robin just minutes after beginning the search. It had Robin's instant attention, though, as he eagerly followed the dog down the slope to an exposed hand.

Keno had detected human scent and dug down and uncovered the glove. With a firm grip, he had pulled the glove off and then run to Robin with his prize, eyes dancing, tail wagging, his mouth almost in a grin, now filled with his new trophy. Keno knew he had done well from the excited reaction erupting from the rescuers. He then led Robin downslope to the exposed hand in the snow. It didn't take long to uncover Ryan's face. Yells of "Over here! We found him and he's still alive!" echoed over the slope. Although not breathing when first exposed to the fresh air, Ryan revived quickly and began breathing on his own. He was suddenly conscious of his surroundings and amazed that he was still alive. The memory of that harrowing experience would be with him a long while.

The enormity of what had just happened was not lost on his rescuers. Robin's first response was incredible relief at finding Ryan alive when the odds were so against it. There was no question that Keno's quick response in searching the deposit was responsible for this unlikely outcome. Minutes or seconds could mean the difference between life and death. People are found alive after being buried for 25 minutes, which was how long it took to find Ryan once he was caught in the slide, but without Keno it was unlikely that there would have been triumph on that particular day. There was little doubt that Ryan had taken the right action that led to being found so quickly. He was buried about 30 centimetres down, but his upthrust hand was near the surface, giving Keno a pool of scent that he easily detected. Robin also thought that Ryan might have created a snow pocket that added to his oxygen supply, and that the amount of available oxygen in the light new snow may have also made a difference.

　· After Ryan was taken to the hospital for observation and treatment for possible hypothermia, the patrollers had a chance to take in what had happened. After the initial relief, they also began to realize that Keno was responsible for the first live recovery of a person by an avalanche-trained search dog in Canada. People had been dug up alive on many occasions by the people in their immediate party, especially when victims were equipped with avalanche beacons, because the rescuers were right there and could begin an immediate search. Though Keno was not at the site when the avalanche occurred, he was at his work station on the hill and could respond much more quickly than a dog team located miles away. But even with that quick response, Ryan was lucky to have survived as long as he did. As lead patroller, Robin felt responsible for the safety of everyone on the hill and knew that this situation could have turned out much worse. Now, he had a dog that was a hero and would be rewarded as such. That night, Keno enjoyed a large steak cooked just the way he liked it—a little underdone.

That was not the end of the honours, however. That year, Keno was awarded the Service Dog of the Year award from the Purina Animal Hall of Fame. Both Robin and Ryan went to Toronto to receive the medal at a ceremony held at the Liberty Grand Entertainment Centre. Robin was also given a plaque and a hand-painted portrait of Keno. This was a special honour for Keno, as previous recipients were police service dogs that had died in the line of duty. Keno was very much alive and quite enjoyed the ceremony.

Keno died seven years later at the age of 12, a ripe old age for working dogs of that size. Though the occasion was sad, Robin felt further honoured when, at a brief dedication, a memorial to the dog was erected at the top of Shakey's Acres ski run. Now, ski hills throughout western Canada have CARDA-trained dog teams on location—a legacy helped along by the yellow dog named Keno.

The History
of Working Dogs

DOGS HAVE SERVED HUMANS FOR centuries in different
capacities. It is not known when humans first tamed wild
dogs, but over time we have taken advantage of their intel-
ligence and loyalty. Anthropologists have noted that dogs
similar to the present-day German shepherd were in use as
far back as 8,000 years ago.

Over this long period of time, people developed many
breeds to meet a variety of demands, isolating and enhanc-
ing each breed's characteristics. Some dogs were bred for
hunting, others for fighting, some for speed or retrieving
and some for herding. But perhaps the bravest dogs are the
working dogs used for search and rescue or police work.

Avalanche Dogs

Bernard of Menthon, a monk of the Augustinian order who later became St. Bernard, is credited with establishing the world's first mountain rescue organization. In the 10th century, he founded a monastery high in the Swiss Alps to provide accommodation and food for weary travellers and pilgrims on their difficult passage through the mountains. Soon, the Augustinian and other religious orders built hospices in strategic locations throughout the Alps, and almost every major pass had a hospice at its summit. These hospices played a critical role in the commerce and travel of the country. In the 18th century, it wasn't uncommon for the St. Bernard Hospice alone to serve 400 meals a day.

By the early 15th century, it was the duty of the resident monks at these hospices to guide travellers up the passes during the winter months. Every morning, a monk would drop down into the valley on either side of the pass to meet the people at a staging area, usually an inn or hut, and guide them up to the pass. Despite this service, a few people travelling alone or lagging behind died every winter from exposure or avalanches.

In the latter half of the 17th century, the monks at the St. Bernard Hospice began to take dogs on their daily sorties over the mountain passes. The dogs were there not just for company, but also for their ability to cut a track through deep snow. They probably could also scent a hard-packed human trail beneath the fresh snow and follow it ahead of the monks. These dogs, which were later named after the St. Bernard Hospice, are likely the forerunners of avalanche search and rescue dogs.

At the hospice, the St. Bernard dogs began their rescue activities spontaneously. When a monk was out looking for people in foggy or stormy conditions, the dogs soon realized the purpose of the exercise. Once they had picked up the scent of the missing traveller, they would lead their master to them. It was a small step from this to smelling out people who had fallen from exhaustion and become lightly covered with snow—and from that to locating people shallowly buried in an avalanche.

However, it is another breed of dog that can be credited with initiating a more formal avalanche-dog program. In the winter of 1937–38, a group on a ski tour in Switzerland was buried in an avalanche. All the victims but one had been found. While the rescuers were searching, someone noticed that a terrier belonging to one of the group kept returning to the same place. This area had already been probed, so no one attached any significance to the dog's actions until it began to bark and whine. The rescuers reprobed the area and found the dog's owner, still alive.

This incident took place at an opportune time because more and more people were frequenting the mountains. When dog expert Ferdinand Schmutz heard about the terrier's performance, he proposed that dogs could be trained to find avalanche victims. The Swiss Army was interested and asked that attempts be made at once to train some dogs. Four German shepherds were duly trained and presented to the army.

After the Second World War, the Swiss Alpine Club organized training courses after becoming interested in having dogs for its own rescue network. Later, other dog clubs in the Alps entered into the activity. Now, the training of avalanche dogs has become so widespread that courses are run all over Europe, North America and all other alpine nations of the world.

Possibly the first documented case of dog finding a missing person in the Canadian Rockies happened inauspiciously in Jasper in 1929. When a warden had not reported in for several days, a group rode in to investigate, with one warden bringing his terrier. As they neared the cabin, the dog started digging in a half metre of freshly fallen snow and uncovered the warden's body. He'd been mauled to death by a grizzly bear.

Police Dogs

Dogs were not formally trained in police work until the 20th century. The French and Germans began experimenting with using dogs for police work in 1895. The well-rounded German shepherd was their breed of choice, but they had no formal training program. It was the Belgians who established a permanent training site for police dogs. The program attracted wide attention in Europe. By 1910,

A German Bergwacht search dog and his handler are harnessed ready to sling under a helicopter.

600 towns in Germany used police dogs, and soon most European nations were incorporating dogs into their law enforcement programs. In North America, New York City was the first to develop a police-dog program, in 1907.

War brought the dogs' skills and natural abilities into focus, and early use of dogs in combat situations often displayed their courage, reliability and loyalty. They searched battlefields for wounded soldiers, guarded buildings and compounds, ran messages along the battlefronts from unit to unit and participated in hand-to-hand combat.

At the beginning of the First World War, Germany had roughly 6,000 trained dogs in service, but the Allies had none. However, as the war continued, a "British War Dog School" was established. Dogs and their handlers were put through a three-month course that included mock battles complete with gas and simulated war sounds such as rifle fire and exploding shells. The simulated battles also included barbed wire, smoke and as much confusion as possible. As a result, England and France were using dogs extensively by the war's end.

After the war, a public memorial honouring war dogs was erected at Kilburn, England. The inscription read in part: "This building is dedicated as a memorial to the countless thousands of God's humble creatures who suffered and perished in the Great War of 1914–1918 knowing nothing of the cause but looking forward to final victory, filled with only love, faith and loyalty, they endured much and died for us."

By the Second World War, all the major powers were using trained dogs. The Germans had founded military kennels in 1934 and had 50,000 dogs in service by September 1939. It wasn't until 1942, though, that the United States began training dogs for military use.

Today, the United Nations also uses dogs in its peacekeeping forces to help prevent insurgency, infiltration and sabotage. And since 9/11, there has been an increased demand for explosives-trained dogs in the fight against terrorism.

Working Dogs in Canada

Canadian law enforcement agencies have been using dogs for public safety purposes since the mid-1890s. Initially, they used sled dogs for transportation between communities and for patrolling. These sled dogs did not perform police work such as apprehending criminals, but they were invaluable in a country as large and underpopulated as Canada— especially in the North.

In Alberta, the provincial police started a modest dog program in 1919 that carried on until 1929, when it was disbanded. Shortly thereafter, in 1930, an informal, all-purpose police-dog program was established again in the province. Sergeant John Cawsey, a widely heralded lawman, and his dog, Dale, became ambassadors for the fledgling dog program. When the RCMP took over law enforcement responsibilities for Alberta in 1932, John

became its employee, with Dale as his silent partner. In
1935, the RCMP hired Dale's previous owner, Captain
Harwich, to help train the team. With that, the RCMP
Police Dog Service was born.

In 1937, after witnessing the successes of Dale and one
of his pups, which was being used as an ambulance dog to
search for lost people, the RCMP commissioner decided to
establish a training school for dogs and handlers, the RCMP
Police Dog Training Centre. By 1939, there were 13 RCMP
dog teams across Canada. Today, there are 121 working
teams and a permanent training facility at Innisfail. This
highly regarded program has also spawned three special-
ized training profiles: narcotics, explosives and avalanche
search and rescue. Since 1970, Parks Canada and the RCMP
have worked closely together in the dog-training field.
The RCMP trains Parks Canada's dogs without charge in
exchange for free mountaineering and avalanche training
for its members.

Until 1980, all certified avalanche-dog handlers in
Canada were professionals employed by the RCMP or Parks
Canada. The early successes of Warden Alfie Burstrom and
his dog, Ginger, and RCMP corporal Dale Morino, who
with his dog, Rocky, became the first RCMP-trained dog
team, created a need for more teams. A few of these new dog
handlers in the RCMP and Parks Canada helped form the
Canadian Avalanche Rescue Dog Association (CARDA) in
the early 1980s.

Warden-service dog handlers Darian Sillence, with Jopo (left), and Mike Henderson, with Attila.

CARDA's backbone was a group of highly motivated dog handlers involved in the ski industry. However, they lacked credibility and needed help with dog training and establishing a high-end training standard. After perseverance and time, and under the tutelage of RCMP and Parks Canada dog handlers, a handful of certified handlers emerged within CARDA. They are now a well-accepted resource used in the field by search and rescue personnel. Today, CARDA provides a valuable service to ski areas, backcountry lodges, heli-ski operations and provincial search and rescue groups, as well as assisting the RCMP and Parks Canada.

Stories about working dogs in Canada come from all corners of the country. These dogs are devoted to their handlers and dedicated to their work. They love to please, and their biggest reward is a small measure of praise. They find children lost in the woods and people buried in avalanches. They can track a person through the thickest bush or across the barest asphalt. They will take a criminal down with no hesitation and are fearless of any threatening weapon. They are our silent heroes.

Index

Index

Acknowledgements

The author acknowledges the following sources for historical reference in this book: the enlightened work of Colin Fraser and his book *The Avalanche Enigma*; the Royal Canadian Mounted Police handout *History of the Police Dog Service*; Parks Canada's *Dog Training Standards for Canadian Parks Service Search and Rescue Dogs*; and the American Alpine Club's *Accidents of North America*. "The Healy Creek Avalanche" was first published in my book *Guardians of the Peaks: Mountain Rescue in the Canadian Rockies and Columbia Mountains*, co-authored with Kathy Calvert and published by Rocky Mountain Books. I would also like to acknowledge the helpful contribution of the following individuals: Alfie Burstrom, Ed Burstrom, Tom Davidson, Pete Ford, Peter Fuhrmann, Bill Hamilton, Olie Hermanrude, Art Laurenson, Gordon McClain, Don Mickle, Gordon Peyto, Jay Pugh, Willi Pfisterer, Rick Ralf, Mike Schintz, Earl Skjonsberg, Jim Sime and Scott Ward. In particular, I want to thank Scott for his critical analysis of the stories and his support and encouragement throughout the writing process. Lastly, I would like to thank my wife, Kathy, for her insight into the world of working dogs, her mountaineering acumen and her editorial critique of this book.

About the Author

Dale Portman is a retired park warden who spent nearly 30 years working for the warden service, often involved with backcountry travel, mountain rescue and avalanche control work in Jasper, Banff, Yoho and Glacier/Revelstoke national parks. He and his wife, Kathy Calvert, live in Cochrane, Alberta, and head to the mountains as often as possible. Dale has written two other books about his experiences working in the mountains of western Canada: *Riding on the Wild Side: Tales of Adventure in the Canadian West* and *Guardians of the Peaks: Mountain Rescue in the Canadian Rockies and Columbia Mountains*, the latter co-written with Kathy. Besides seeing new cultures in foreign lands, Dale's greatest love is for extended trips to remote parts of the Canadian Rockies, by skis, on foot or on horseback leading a couple of pack horses.

More Great Books in the Amazing Stories Series

Riding on the Wild Side

Tales of Adventure in the Canadian West

Dale Portman

(ISBN 978-1-894974-80-6)

Park warden Dale Portman lived his dream of riding the range for a living in the spectacular Canadian Rockies. His exhilarating tales take us to an Old West world of wild horses and hair-raising roundups, youthful bravado and larger-than-life characters: Bert, the tough Millarville patriarch; Donny and Faye, free-spirited children of the Alberta foothills; and Jim, the eccentric English park warden who careens from one potential disaster to another. Filled with humour and adventure, these true stories capture the excitement and danger of backcountry life.

Visit www.heritagehouse.ca to see the entire list of books in this series.